MANAGEMENT INFORMATION SYSTEM

Practical Insights and Applications in Indonesia

(2nd Edition)

Andy Ismail
Dr. Rike Setiawati
Herzalina Herbenita
Bambang Sutejo
Sigit Mulyanto
Muhammad Aqshal Zorif
Mustika Sari
Uswatun Hasanah
Della Adelia
Ghani Akbar

DEDICATION

This book is dedicated to all the passionate and aspiring minds who seek to transform the world through the power of information and technology. To our families, whose unwavering support and encouragement have been our constant source of strength. To our mentors and colleagues, who have guided and inspired us through every step of our journey. And to the students of Universitas Jambi, whose enthusiasm for learning and innovation drives us to push the boundaries of knowledge and understanding.

May this book serve as a beacon of knowledge and inspiration, lighting the path for future generations of innovators and leaders in the field of management information systems. We hope it empowers you to harness the potential of technology to create meaningful and lasting impacts in your organizations and communities.

With heartfelt gratitude and dedication,

Andy Ismail, Dr. Rike Setiawati, Herzalina Herbenita, Bambang Sutejo, Sigit Mulyanto, Muhammad Aqshal Zorif, Mustika Sari, Uswatun Hasanah, Della Adelia, and Ghani Akbar

CONTENTS

CHAPTER 1: MARKETING INFORMATION SYSTEMS & MANUFACTURING INFORMATION SYSTEMS

An information system is a major component in the operation of an organization. It is a collection of various elements, such as people, equipment, procedures, and data. These components work in synergy to collect, process, store and distribute information. The information generated by these systems is a very valuable resource for the organization, and has a variety of benefits that are very meaningful[1].

One of the main roles of information systems is in managing raw material inventory in the company. Raw material inventory is an important element in the supply chain of a company. This supply chain involves various stages, from the procurement of raw materials to the distribution of finished products to consumers. To maintain the smooth running of this process, companies must have an effective information system.

---

[1] Hidayatun, N., Marlina, S., & Adinata, E. (2020). INVENTORY SYSTEM DESIGN FOR RAW MATERIAL INVENTORY DATA MANAGEMENT.

First of all, information systems help companies manage raw material inventory more efficiently. With a good information system, companies can monitor raw material inventory in real-time. This allows companies to avoid inventory shortages that can disrupt production. On the other hand, information systems also help companies avoid excessive inventory buildup, which can erode the company's profits.

In addition, information systems also play a key role in optimizing the purchasing process. With an integrated information system, companies can easily track raw material orders, manage payments to suppliers, and even compare prices from various suppliers. This allows companies to make smarter and more economical purchasing decisions.

Not only in procurement, information systems also help in monitoring the quality of raw materials. With the use of sensor technology and automated monitoring, companies can accurately check the quality of incoming raw materials. This helps in identifying defective products or raw materials that do not meet quality standards. As a result, companies can take immediate action to avoid distributing defective products to the market.

Furthermore, information systems also support production planning. Proper production planning requires a deep understanding of available raw material inventory, production capacity, and market demand. Information systems provide visibility into all these aspects. With accurate data, companies can plan production efficiently, avoid inventory shortages or buildups, and ensure that products can be provided as per customer demand.

In the era of globalization and increasingly fierce competition, efficiency and flexibility are essential. Information systems help companies to face these challenges by providing accurate and timely information. With a good information system, companies can respond quickly to market changes, adjust production to demand, and ensure that raw material supplies are always available when needed.

In addition, information systems also support supply chain integration. An efficient supply chain involves close collaboration between companies, suppliers and other partners. Information systems enable companies to share information with their business partners. This creates better coordination in the supply chain, minimizes delays, and reduces the cost of miscommunication.

Finally, information systems also provide powerful data analysis. By collecting and analyzing data regarding raw material inventory management, companies can identify trends, opportunities, and challenges that may arise. This data analysis can help companies make smarter strategic decisions. For example, companies can identify opportunities to optimize their supply chain, streamline production processes, or pursue further cost efficiencies.

Marketing Information System

Marketing Information System (MIS) is a system that has a crucial role in supporting marketing management in making decisions related to planning, implementing, and controlling marketing programs. It is a key element in a company's marketing strategy, which plays a central role in achieving business goals. In this context, it is necessary to deepen the understanding of the role and usefulness of SIP in supporting the marketing process.

According to Kotler and Keller (2016), two leading experts in the marketing world, SIP is a system designed with the primary purpose of collecting, managing, and presenting information that is urgently needed by marketing management.

The information obtained from SIPs is crucial in guiding decisions related to marketing strategy, resource allocation, target market selection, and various other aspects related to marketing. In other words, SIPs are an invaluable source of information for marketing management within a company.[2] .

SIP has several key functions that support various aspects of marketing. One of them is its ability to help companies identify market opportunities. By analyzing the data and information collected, companies can identify market trends, customer preferences, and potential promising market segments. This allows companies to take more appropriate strategic steps in marketing their products or services, which can ultimately increase sales and market share.

More so, SIPs also assist companies in developing effective marketing strategies. By having access to accurate and up-to-date information about the market and competitors, companies can formulate better strategies to compete in the market. This includes the selection of appropriate promotion methods, competitive pricing, and the development of products that suit customer needs.

---

[2] Kotler, P., & Keller, K. L. (2016). Marketing Management. Pearson.

After formulating strategies, SIP also helps in the implementation of marketing programs. This involves using information obtained from the system to plan and launch marketing campaigns, manage product inventory, and organize product distribution. With SIPs, companies can optimize resource allocation and ensure that marketing programs go according to plan.

Controlling marketing performance is also an important aspect of marketing management, and this is again where SIP becomes critical. With the data and reports generated by the system, companies can measure the results of their marketing programs. This includes evaluating whether sales goals have been achieved, whether the ROI (Return on Investment) of the marketing program is positive, and whether there are changes in brand image or customer perception. With this information, management can make the necessary adjustments in their marketing strategies.

Kotler and Keller (2016) clearly state that SIPs are key in making smart marketing decisions. With the right data and information, marketing management can make better decisions, avoid costly mistakes, and respond quickly to market changes. In the competitive business world, the ability to adapt and respond to market changes is invaluable.

Despite the important role of SIPs in marketing management, it is also important to remember that their use must be accompanied by wisdom in safeguarding and protecting customer data. In an era where customer privacy is of increasing concern, companies must secure the information obtained from SIP properly and comply with applicable privacy regulations. Data security is an equally crucial aspect of using a marketing information system.

Marketing Information System Example

There are various Marketing Information System (MIS) software used by companies to support their marketing operations. One globally renowned example is the "Salesforce Marketing Cloud." Salesforce Marketing Cloud is a platform that provides various cloud-based marketing tools that help companies manage campaigns, customer analytics, marketing automation, and social media monitoring. The platform has a large user base and is used by companies all over the world.

Meanwhile, in Indonesia, several local software companies have developed SIP solutions tailored to the needs of the Indonesian market. An obvious example is "Warung Pintar," which is an Indonesian technology company that offers a SIP platform for micro and small businesses (MSMEs) in Indonesia.

Warung Pintar helps MSMEs manage inventory, sales, and reporting more efficiently. With this app, MSMEs in Indonesia can leverage technology to optimize their marketing operations.

In addition, there are also other examples such as "Sirclo." Sirclo is an Indonesian technology company that provides various e-commerce and digital marketing solutions, including a SIP platform that helps companies manage and optimize their online stores. Sirclo allows companies to create an easy-to-manage online store and supports various marketing features, such as promotions, inventory management, and order tracking.

In the face of increasing competition, SIP software developed in Indonesia is increasingly important to help companies develop effective and competitive marketing strategies. With these localized solutions, companies in Indonesia can access marketing tools that suit their market characteristics and business needs. This also supports the growth of MSMEs and the e-commerce industry in Indonesia, which has been growing rapidly in recent years.

Manufacturing Information System

Manufacturing Information System (MIS) is a key foundation in the production process in various companies. MIS plays a role in collecting, processing, and presenting information that is indispensable to production management in making decisions that impact the planning, execution, and control of the production process. The concept of MIS has become a vital element in running efficient and effective production operations.

According to Turban et al. (2005), MIS is a system specifically designed to provide support in collecting, managing, and utilizing production-related information. This information includes data on raw material requirements, production capacity, labor allocation, and other information that is critical to better manage production. MIS assists companies in optimizing production decision-making, overseeing the course of the production process, and controlling overall production performance[3] .

---

[3] Turban, E., Outland, J., King, D., Lee, J., & Liang, T. (2005). Electronic Commerce 2006: A Managerial Perspective. Prentice Hall.

In the book "Manufacturing Planning and Control for Supply Chain Management" 6th edition, Jacobs and Chase (2017) explain how MIS has an important role in supporting various aspects of production. One of them is its ability to optimize the use of resources.

MIS allows companies to better manage inventory and identify available resources. This means that companies can maximize the utilization of the resources they have, including machinery, manpower, and raw material inventory. By allocating resources efficiently, companies can achieve more optimized production and reduce wastage[4] .

Production efficiency is of utmost importance in a manufacturing environment. MIS has a central role in improving production efficiency. By collecting and analyzing production data in real-time, MIS enables companies to identify potential improvements in the production process. From here, companies can implement the necessary process improvements to increase production efficiency. This can involve improvements in work flow, better production scheduling, or the use of more advanced technologies for automation.

---

[4] Jacobs, F. R., & Chase, R. B. (2017). Manufacturing Planning and Control for Supply Chain Management. McGraw-Hill.

In addition, MIS helps companies in reducing production costs. By having better visibility over the production process, companies can identify areas where cost savings can be achieved. This can include reduction of raw material wastage, control of labor costs, and more efficient inventory management. With MIS, companies can conduct more rigorous cost monitoring and take necessary actions to reduce production costs.

Product quality is another aspect that is of great concern in the manufacturing world. MIS can help companies in improving the quality of their products. By analyzing production data, MIS can identify defects or quality issues that may arise during the production process. By quickly identifying these issues, companies can take corrective actions to ensure that the products produced meet the set quality standards.

Manufacturing Information System Example

In the world, there are various Manufacturing Information System (MIS) software that support companies in managing and optimizing their production processes. One example of globally recognized MIS software is "SAP Manufacturing Execution" from SAP, the world's leading software company. The software is designed to assist companies in monitoring and controlling production operations in real-time.

SAP Manufacturing Execution integrates data from various production lines and allows management to make better decisions based on accurate information.

Meanwhile, in Indonesia, several software companies have developed MIS solutions tailored to the needs of the domestic manufacturing industry. An obvious example is "Mitra Integrasi Informatika" (MII), which is an Indonesian technology company that provides various software solutions for the manufacturing industry. MII offers a range of products and services that include production monitoring, inventory management, and production automation. MII's products help manufacturing companies in Indonesia to increase the efficiency of their operations and improve product quality.

In addition, "Petrokimia Gresik," a leading chemical manufacturing company in Indonesia, has developed a MIS software solution tailored to the needs of the chemical industry. The software is designed to monitor and control chemical production processes more efficiently, ensure operation safety, and meet stringent quality standards. Initiatives such as these show how leading Indonesian companies are seeking to leverage information technology to optimize their manufacturing operations.

Not only companies, the Indonesian government has also understood the importance of technology in the manufacturing industry. They have launched various programs and initiatives to support digital transformation in the manufacturing industry. These include incentives and support for companies looking to adopt MIS software to improve their production efficiency.

The use of MIS software that is tailored to the characteristics of industries in Indonesia is essential in facing global challenges and competition. With these local solutions, companies in Indonesia can leverage technology to optimize their production operations, reduce waste, and ensure that the products produced meet strict quality standards. In addition, such initiatives can also help in improving the competitiveness of Indonesia's manufacturing industry in the global market.

In the ever-evolving world of manufacturing, Manufacturing Information System (MIS) software is an invaluable tool. MIS helps companies in improving production efficiency, reducing production costs, and ensuring high product quality. In Indonesia, local initiatives in MIS software development demonstrate a commitment to adopting technology in the manufacturing industry. Through MIS software solutions that suit the needs of the industry in the country, companies in Indonesia can improve their competitiveness in an increasingly tight global market.

CHAPTER 2: HR INFORMATION SYSTEM & ACCOUNTING INFORMATION SYSTEM

HR Information System

Human Resources Information System (HRIS) is the backbone of any organization that focuses on managing human resources. In the growing digital era and globalization, it is important to have an information system that can help companies manage and optimize their human resources.

The HR Information System is an invaluable tool for managing information related to employees in an organization. It covers various important aspects, such as personal data, attendance data, salary data, performance data, and more. With this system, companies can easily access and manage this information efficiently.

One of the key benefits of an HR Information System is its ability to assist in the recruitment and selection process of new employees. The recruitment process is the first step in building a quality team. The system allows companies to better collect, organize, and analyze data on potential employees. Thus, companies can make better recruitment decisions and identify talent that suits their needs.

Not only that, the HR Information System also provides solutions for employee training and development. Human resource management is not only about recruiting and hiring employees but also about developing their potential. With this system, companies can track the training and development that has been provided to each employee. This helps in ensuring that the employee keeps improving his skills and knowledge according to the demands of the job.

Talent management is another important aspect managed by HR Information Systems. Companies often have talented employees who need to be identified and managed properly. The system allows companies to better track the potential and performance of employees. With accurate data, companies can take appropriate actions to promote and develop such talent.

However, the benefits of HR Information Systems are not limited to the employee management aspect. With this system, companies can also manage financial aspects related to HR, such as payroll and human resource expense management. This increases efficiency and accuracy in the employee salary payment process.

HR Information Systems also provide benefits in terms of decision making. With properly collected and processed data, HR managers can make more accurate and fact-based decisions. This helps in improving the overall efficiency and effectiveness of HR management.

In addition to these benefits, HR Information Systems also help in improving the quality of HR-related data. With accurate and up-to-date data, companies can avoid mistakes that may occur in human resource management. Accurate data also helps in ensuring transparency and accountability in all HR processes.

When we refer to the book "Management Information Systems" by Raymond McLeod and George Schell, they underline the importance of HR Information Systems in improving the efficiency, effectiveness and accuracy of HR management. This also has an impact on increasing transparency and accountability, which is very important in managing human resources well[5] .

---

[5] McLeod, R., & Schell, G. (2007). Management Information Systems. Fourth Edition.

Human Resources Information System is a strong foundation for managing human resources in an organization. With its ability to manage employee data, assist with recruitment and selection processes, employee training and development, and talent management, this system provides significant added value to the company.

By utilizing advanced HR technology and information systems, companies can manage human resources more effectively, efficiently, and accurately, contributing positively to their long-term success.

HR Information System Example

There are several examples of software that can be used to manage employee data in a company. Here are some examples of software for human resource management:

1. gtHR HR Software: This software is designed for Human Resource Information System that helps to simplify the workflow in a company's human resource management activities. The main features of the software include managing employee data, recruitment, and employee attendance[6].

---

[6] https://blog.gamatechno.com/7-software-hr-terbaik-untuk-sistem-informasi-kepegawaian/?amp=1

2. Dokodemo-Kerja: This is a comprehensive Human Resource Information System that can help manage employee data, including attendance, leave, and performance. The software is available in the form of a website or mobile application[7].

3. AskaraHR: This software can help manage employee administration, leave reports, attendance, employee performance, and salary calculations[8].

4. Zoho People: This cloud-based software can help streamline HR processes, including the management of employee data, attendance, and leave. The software also uses a centralized database to store employee records from all departments in one location[9].

5. Accurate: This software can help manage employee data, including attendance, leave, and salary calculations. It also provides performance management and recruitment features[10].

These software examples can be used as a reference for companies that want to implement a human resource management system. By using the appropriate software, companies can optimize employee data management and improve efficiency in their HR activities.

---

[7] https://dokodemo-kerja.com/blog/ind/info-hrd/sistem-informasi-sumber-daya-man usia/

[8] https://askarasoft.com/aplikasi-departement-sdm/

[9] https://dokodemo-kerja.com/blog/ind/info-hris/software-hr/

[10] https://accurate.id/marketing-manajemen/sistem-informasi-sdm/

Accounting Information System

Accounting Information System (AIS) is a system that collects, records, stores, and processes accounting data to produce useful information for decision makers. AIS assists companies in managing financial transactions and providing reports needed by management, investors, regulators, and other external parties. AIS consists of various components, including hardware, software, procedures, data, and the people who use the system [11] [12].

Functions and Benefits of Accounting Information Systems

1. Improve Accuracy and Efficiency: AIS enables automation of accounting processes, such as recording transactions, calculating taxes, and generating financial reports. This reduces the risk of human error and speeds up the accounting process.

2. Timely Information Provision: With AIS, financial reports can be generated in real-time, allowing management to make decisions based on current and relevant information.

3. Internal Control Enhancement: AIS provides effective internal control mechanisms, such as access restrictions, audit trails, and data validation, which help in detecting and preventing fraud or abuse.

---

[11] Romney, M.B., & Steinbart, P.J. (2015). Accounting Information Systems (13th ed.). Pearson Education.
[12] Hall, J.A. (2016). Accounting Information Systems (9th ed.). Cengage Learning.

4. Facilitating Compliance: SIAs ensure that companies comply with applicable regulations and accounting standards by producing financial statements that are compliant with regulatory requirements.

5. Cost Savings: By reducing manual work and increasing efficiency, AIS helps companies save on operational costs.

Key Components of Accounting Information Systems

1. Hardware: Computers, servers, scanners, and other devices used to input, process, and store accounting data.

2. Software: Accounting applications used to manage financial data, such as ERP (Enterprise Resource Planning) software and specialized accounting applications such as QuickBooks or MYOB.

3. Data: Accounting information inputted into the system, including financial transactions, customer records, and inventory.

4. Procedures and Policies: Steps to be followed in recording and reporting transactions, as well as policies governing the use of and access to the system.

5. People: AIS users, including accountants, financial managers, and administrative staff, who are responsible for inputting data and using the information generated by the system.

Processes in Accounting Information System

1. Data Collection: Transaction data is collected through various sources, such as sales invoices, purchase receipts, and general journals.

2. Recording: Data collected is recorded in journals and ledgers using appropriate accounting methods.

3. Processing: The recorded data is processed to produce financial statements, such as balance sheets, income statements, and cash flow statements.

4. Storage: Accounting data is stored in a secure database and can be accessed as needed.

5. Reporting: Information generated by the AIS is presented in the form of financial statements that are used by management and other external parties.

Challenges in Implementing Accounting Information Systems

1. Implementation Costs: AIS implementation can require a significant initial investment, including hardware, software, and training costs.

2. Training Needs: AIS users need to be trained to be able to use the system effectively and understand the related procedures.

3. Data Security: Protection of sensitive accounting data is a major challenge, including threats from hackers and the risk of data loss.

4. Integration with Other Systems: AIS should be integrated with other information systems in the company, such as inventory management systems and human resource management systems, to ensure data consistency and accuracy.

Case Study of Accounting Information System Implementation

PT XYZ:

PT XYZ is a manufacturing company that faces problems in financial management because it still uses manual processes. By implementing ERP-based AIS, PT XYZ managed to improve operational efficiency, reduce recording errors, and provide faster and more accurate financial reports.

ABC store:

Toko ABC is a small business that has difficulty in managing sales and inventory transactions. By using simple yet effective accounting software, Toko ABC can monitor sales, manage inventory, and generate monthly financial reports more easily.

Accounting Information System is a very important tool for companies in managing and reporting financial information. By automating accounting processes, AIS helps improve accuracy, efficiency, and regulatory compliance. Although there are challenges in its implementation, the benefits provided by AIS make it a worthwhile investment for companies of any size.

CHAPTER 3: FINANCIAL INFORMATION SYSTEMS

The implementation of financial information systems may vary depending on the size of the organization, the industry in which it operates, and its specific needs. There are various approaches that organizations can take in implementing a financial information system, and these can include developing a system tailored to their specific needs, adopting an off-the-shelf solution, or leveraging cloud-based services[13]. However, the most important thing is to choose a system that matches the organization's requirements and can be easily integrated into existing processes and workflows.

In the case of customized financial information system development, the organization has full control over the design and development of the system. This allows them to ensure that the system built fully meets their needs. In addition, the system built can be well integrated with other systems used in the organization. However, the development of a customized system also requires significant resources, both in terms of time and cost. In addition, organizations need to have a skilled IT team to manage and support these systems.

---

[13] Nadia Kurniati, A., & Devitra, J. (2022). Web-based Student Financial Administration Information System at Yadika High School, Jambi City. Journal of Information Systems Management.

On the other hand, organizations that do not have sufficient resources or technical expertise may choose to adopt off-the-shelf solutions. Off-the-shelf solutions have generally been developed by software vendors and can be quickly implemented. However, organizations need to ensure that the solution can meet their needs and can be integrated with their existing systems. Selection of the right solution is critical in this regard, and organizations need to conduct a thorough evaluation before adopting a particular solution.

In addition, many organizations today are also considering the utilization of cloud-based services for their financial information systems. Cloud computing allows organizations to access their systems and data from anywhere with an internet connection. This can provide greater flexibility in terms of access and scalability. However, it is important to ensure that financial data stored in the cloud is secure and well protected.

In all of the above approaches, the key factor is to ensure that the selected financial information system can meet the needs of the organization. This involves a deep understanding of the business processes and specific needs of the organization. Before making a decision, organizations need to conduct a careful and thorough analysis of what they need from their financial information system. This involves communicating with various departments and stakeholders in the organization to understand their needs.

In addition, the integration of the financial information system into existing processes and workflows is also a key factor. The system should be able to operate seamlessly with other systems used in the organization. This can speed up processes and improve operational efficiency.

Furthermore, organizations need to consider the aspect of information security. Financial data is highly sensitive and must be properly protected. This includes adopting best practices in terms of data security, as well as ensuring that the systems used have strong access controls.

During the implementation process, good training is also very important. Users of financial information systems need to be given sufficient training to ensure that they can use the system effectively. This can reduce human error and ensure that the system is used in the best way possible.

The implementation of a financial information system is an important step in supporting the financial operations of an organization. This process should be carefully considered, with a focus on selecting a system that suits the organization's needs and can be integrated well within existing workflows. With the right approach, financial information system implementation can help organizations improve efficiency, accuracy, and security in managing their financial data.

The implementation of a financial information system has several benefits. First, it improves decision-making through better access and more in-depth analysis of financial data[14]. Second, efficiency and accuracy in financial reporting and management are significantly improved[15]. In addition, the system also increases accountability and transparency within the organization[16]. Lastly, financial processes become more efficient and manual errors are reduced[17].

However, there are several challenges that organizations may face when implementing a financial information system. The first challenge is integration with existing systems and processes[18]. Secondly, it is important to ensure that the selected system meets the specific needs and requirements of the organization[19].

---

[14] Riadi, B., Yusman, M., & Utami, Y.T. (2021). WEB-BASED FINANCIAL INFORMATION SYSTEM FOR VILLAGE-OWNED ENTERPRISES (BUMDES) TUNAS MANDIRI DESA NEGARA RATU. Pepadun Journal.

[15] Nadia Kurniati, A., & Devitra, J. (2022). Web-based Student Financial Administration Information System at Yadika High School, Jambi City. Journal of Information Systems Management.

[16] Gunawan, P.D., Animah, A., & Isnawati, I. (2022). Financial Information Systems in Improving Village Accountability. E-Journal of Accounting.

[17] Sri, S.W. (2022). FINANCIAL ACCOUNTING INFORMATION SYSTEM TO ANALYZE THE HEALTH OF WEB-BASED COMPANIES. Compact: Scientific Journal of Accounting Computerization.

[18] Warisaji, T.T., & Rosyidah, U.A. (2022). Design of Financial Information System for Monitoring and Evaluation of Cooperatives. BIOS: Journal of Information Technology and Computer Engineering.

[19] Nadia Kurniati, A., & Devitra, J. (2022). Web-based Student Financial Administration Information System at Yadika High School, Jambi City. Journal of Information Systems Management.

In addition, training and support for users who may not be familiar with the new system is crucial. The final challenge is ongoing maintenance and updates to ensure the system remains relevant and up-to-date[20].

Example of a Financial Information System

The implementation of financial information systems has brought about many positive changes in different types of organizations. Here are some examples of well-known and widely used financial information systems in various industries:

1. SAP Financial Accounting (SAP FI): SAP FI is part of the SAP ERP module that is used by many large companies around the world to manage various aspects of their finances. This module provides features such as general ledger management, fixed assets, accounts payable and receivable, and financial reporting. SAP FI enables seamless integration with other SAP modules, such as controlling, material management, and sales & distribution, thus enabling high visibility and consistency of data across the organization.

---

[20] Sri, S.W. (2022). FINANCIAL ACCOUNTING INFORMATION SYSTEM TO ANALYZE THE HEALTH OF WEB-BASED COMPANIES. Compact: Scientific Journal of Accounting Computerization.

2. Oracle Financials: Oracle Financials is part of the Oracle E-Business Suite that offers a complete solution for managing company finances. Key features include general ledger management, cash management, accounts payable and receivable management, and financial analytics. Oracle Financials is designed to help companies improve operational efficiency, optimize financial performance, and comply with applicable financial regulations.

3. QuickBooks: QuickBooks is an accounting software that is popular among small and medium-sized businesses. QuickBooks provides features such as transaction recording, expense tracking, invoice management, and financial reporting. With a user-friendly interface, QuickBooks allows users with no accounting background to easily manage their finances.

4. Microsoft Dynamics 365 Finance: Microsoft Dynamics 365 Finance is part of the Dynamics 365 suite that integrates financial functions with other business processes, such as supply chain management and human resources. The system offers advanced analytics capabilities, financial process automation, and support for multiple currencies and international regulations. It helps companies to gain better insight into their financial performance and make more informed decisions.

5. Xero: Xero is a cloud-based accounting software that is widely used by small and medium-sized businesses. Xero offers features such as expense tracking, bank reconciliation, invoice management, and financial reporting. Xero's strengths are its ability to be accessed from anywhere, anytime, as well as integration with various third-party applications to extend its functionality.

CHAPTER 4: INFORMATION SYSTEM DESIGN

Introduction to Information System Design

In detailing how vital information system design is, we can understand that this process has a significant impact on the operational effectiveness and efficiency of an organization. Information system design paves the way for the creation of an organized and unified structure, facilitating the smooth flow of information across organizational entities. Therefore, understanding the needs and objectives of information system design is crucial to come up with a solution that suits the dynamics and complexity of the organization.

The process of designing information systems involves structured stages, starting with requirements analysis. In this stage, an in-depth understanding of the organization's needs becomes the main foundation. The identification of these needs includes an analysis of the business processes, user needs, and strategic goals of the company. The results of this analysis form the basis for designing a system that can provide solutions that are relevant and appropriate to the organizational context.

Furthermore, information system design includes a design phase that focuses on detailing the system structure technically and functionally. Technical design involves selecting the right infrastructure and planning the implementation of supporting technologies. Meanwhile, the functional design specifies how the system will interact with users and how data will be processed. The synergy between technical and functional design is key to creating an information system that is not only technologically efficient, but also in line with user needs and preferences.

The next step is implementation, where the design that has been compiled is realized into a running information system. This stage involves coding, testing, and integration of system components. Testing plays a critical role in ensuring system reliability, detecting potential bugs, and ensuring that the system operates as intended. Along with that, users are also involved in this stage to ensure the system can be used easily and according to their expectations.

After implementation, the next step is the operation stage. The information system that has been implemented must be able to function consistently and effectively in supporting the daily activities of the organization. System maintenance is also a critical aspect in this operation stage, ensuring that the system can continue to adapt to changing needs and technology.

In the whole process of designing an information system, it is important to continuously consider the aspect of information security. Information security is a determining factor in maintaining data integrity, confidentiality and availability. Therefore, the integration of appropriate security protocols and access policies becomes an integral part of effective information system design and implementation.

Overall, an in-depth understanding of information system design has significant implications for organizational progress. By detailing the steps, organizations can ensure that the information systems implemented not only meet operational needs, but are also able to adapt to the ever-changing dynamics in the business environment.

The definition and purpose of information system design summarizes the process of creating a system that aims to manage, organize, and access information to improve effectiveness, efficiency, and accuracy in various work processes.

Here are some concrete examples that reflect the purpose and definition of information system design.

1. Information System for Purchasing, Selling, and Distributing Accura Ceramics. The purpose of this system is to design a website-based platform for purchasing, selling, and distributing Accura ceramics. This system focuses on solving problems related to ordering Accura ceramics by making it easy for customers to place orders through an online platform. In addition, this system also ensures that order information can be accessed quickly and accurately by the admin[21].

2. Tofu Sales Information System. This system aims to create a Java-based desktop application with MySQL database to facilitate the tofu sales process in a factory. By using this system, it is expected to increase operational effectiveness and efficiency, including the presentation of timely reports for company owners. Thus, the design of this system has a positive impact on the sales management and reporting process[22].

---

[21] debbyanti, F. (2013). Information System for Purchasing, Sales, and Distribution of accura ceramics based on Website at PT SAMAJAYASUKSESABADI.

[22] Wahyudin, I., Natsir, F., & Vandini, I. (2022). Design of Tofu Sales Information System Application at UG Pariangan Tofu Factory based on Java. Journal of Information Technology and Management Applications (JATIM).

3. Purchasing and Sales Management Information System. This system is designed with the aim of assisting company leaders in monitoring overall performance, including monitoring purchase prices, purchases, and sales. Through this system, company leaders can easily access the information needed for more effective decision making. Thus, this system becomes an efficient tool in supporting the company's management functions [23][24].

4. Medical Check-Up Information System. Designing a patient data information system to provide more effective information related to registration and examination schedules at medical check-up clinics. This system helps improve efficiency in the clinic's administrative process, with a dynamic knowledge base that supports patient data management. Thus, this system aims to improve the accuracy and effectiveness of health services [25].

[23] Muhairia, A., & Novitarina, D.A. (2010). SALES, PURCHASE AND INVENTORY MANAGEMENT INFORMATION SYSTEM AT PT. ROMINDO PALEMBANG.

[24] Sani, A., & Ratih, R. (2010). MANAGEMENT INFORMATION SYSTEM OF SALES, INVENTORY AND PURCHASING AT PT. KARYA SUKA ABADI PALEMBANG.

[25] Rifai, M., & Sarono, J. (2014). Information System for Medical Check Up CTKI Klinik Mitra Mutiara. Journal of CoSciTech (Computer Science and Information Technology).

In each instance, the primary goal of information system design is to improve effectiveness, efficiency, and accuracy in the organization's work processes. System design steps, such as requirements analysis, system design, coding, testing, operation, and maintenance phases, are integral in achieving this goal.

Definition of information system design and its relationship with organizational goals.

Information system design is a process that involves identifying needs, analyzing, and creating a system that meets the specific needs of the organization. The main objective of information system design is to ensure that the system built can support the operations and strategic goals of the organization effectively and efficiently.

The process of designing an information system begins with a needs analysis, which involves an in-depth understanding of the organization's business processes, user needs, and strategic objectives. Once the needs are identified, the next step is to design a technical solution that can meet those needs. This includes the selection of appropriate hardware and software, as well as the design of procedures and policies to be used in the system.

The relationship between information system design and organizational goals is very close. Well-designed information systems can help organizations achieve their goals by providing accurate and timely data, improving operational efficiency, and supporting better decision making. For example, by using effective information systems, management can gain better insight into the performance of the organization and thus can make more informed decisions to achieve their strategic goals. In addition, a good information system can also increase the organization's flexibility in responding to changes in the market and business environment.

Laudon and Laudon suggest that information system design is a process consisting of various stages, from needs analysis to system implementation and maintenance. Each stage must be carried out carefully to ensure that the resulting system can meet the needs of the organization and contribute to the achievement of their strategic goals. This shows that designing information systems is not just about technology, but also about understanding how technology can be used to support overall business goals[26] .

---

[26] Laudon, K.C., & Laudon, J.P. (2018). Management Information Systems: Managing the Digital Firm (15th ed.). Pearson.

Thus, the design of information systems has a significant impact on the success of organizations in achieving their goals. By ensuring that the information systems designed can support business operations and strategic objectives, organizations can improve their efficiency, effectiveness, and flexibility in facing challenges and opportunities in the market.

Information System Design Steps and Methodology

Information system design requires a systematic and structured approach in order to produce a system that meets the needs of the organization and supports the achievement of strategic goals. The following are the steps and methodologies commonly used in designing information systems:

1. Needs Analysis

The first step in designing an information system is to conduct a needs analysis. This process involves gathering information from various sources, such as interviews with users, surveys, observations, and analysis of existing documents. The purpose of the needs analysis is to deeply understand the organization's business processes, information needs, and problems faced by current users. The results of this needs analysis will be the basis for designing a system that suits the needs of the organization[27] .

---

[27] Laudon, K.C., & Laudon, J.P. (2018). Management Information Systems: Managing the Digital Firm (15th ed.). Pearson.

2. System Planning

Once the needs are identified, the next step is system planning. This planning includes determining the scope of the project, allocating resources, and scheduling design activities. At this stage, the methodology to be used for system design and development is also determined. Frequently used methodologies include Waterfall, Agile, and Spiral.

3. System Design

The system design stage involves creating a conceptual design and detailed design of the information system. Conceptual design includes modeling of business processes, data flows, and data structures. The detailed design includes technical specifications, such as system architecture, database design, user interface design, and software specifications. At this stage, the technology to be used in system development is also selected.

4. Development and Implementation

In the development stage, the information system is built according to the design that has been made. This process involves coding, unit testing, integration, and system testing. After the system is developed, the implementation stage is carried out by installing the system in the production environment, configuring the system, and training users. This stage also involves migrating data from the old system to the new system, if required.

5. Testing and Validation

Testing and validation are carried out to ensure that the system built functions according to specifications and meets user needs. Testing includes functional testing, performance testing, security testing, and user acceptance testing. Validation is done by involving users in system testing to ensure that the system meets their expectations and can be used in daily operations.

6. Maintenance and Evaluation

After the system is implemented, a maintenance phase is performed to ensure that the system continues to function properly and can adjust to changing business and technology needs. Maintenance includes bug fixes, system upgrades, and adjustments to changes in regulations or organizational policies. System evaluations are conducted periodically to assess system performance and determine if there is a need for system upgrades or replacement.

Information System Design Steps and Methodology

```
                            ●
                            │
                            ▼
              ┌─────────────────────────┐       ┌──────────────────────────────┐
              │  Conduct Needs Analysis  │───────│ Input: Information from       │
              └─────────────────────────┘       │ interviews, surveys,          │
                            │                    │ observations, and             │
                            │                    │ existing documents.           │
                            │                    │ Output: Understanding of      │
                            │                    │ business processes,           │
                            │                    │ information needs,            │
                            ▼                    │ and user problems.            │
              ┌─────────────────────────┐       └──────────────────────────────┘
              │     System Planning      │───────┌──────────────────────────────┐
              └─────────────────────────┘       │ Input: Needs analysis results.│
                            │                    │ Output: Project scope,        │
                            │                    │ resource allocation, and      │
                            ▼                    │ design activity schedule.     │
      ┌──────────────────────────────┐           └──────────────────────────────┘
      │ Determine Design Methodology │
      └──────────────────────────────┘
                            │
                            ▼
              ┌─────────────────────────┐       ┌──────────────────────────────┐
              │      System Design       │───────│ Input: System planning        │
              └─────────────────────────┘       │ details.                      │
                            │                    │ Output: Conceptual design,    │
                            │                    │ detailed design, technical    │
                            ▼                    │ specifications.               │
      ┌──────────────────────────────┐           └──────────────────────────────┘
      │ Select Technology for Development │
      └──────────────────────────────┘
                            │
                            ▼
          ┌──────────────────────────────┐   ┌──────────────────────────────┐
          │ Development and Implementation │───│ Input: Detailed design and    │
          └──────────────────────────────┘   │ technical specifications.     │
                            │                  │ Output: Developed system,     │
                            │                  │ installed system,             │
                            ▼                  │ trained users.                │
              ┌─────────────────────────┐     └──────────────────────────────┘
              │   Testing and Validation │───────┌──────────────────────────────┐
              └─────────────────────────┘       │ Input: Developed system.      │
                            │                    │ Output: Validated system that │
                            │                    │ meets specifications and      │
                            ▼                    │ user needs.                   │
            yes ◇ System Meets Specifications? ◇ no └───────────────────────────┘
           ▼                              ▼
┌──────────────────────────┐   ┌──────────────────────────┐
│ Proceed to Maintenance   │   │ Rework and Conduct        │
│ and Evaluation           │   │ Additional Testing and    │
└──────────────────────────┘   │ Validation                │
           │                    └──────────────────────────┘
           │                              │
           │                              ▼
           │                   ┌──────────────────────────┐
           │                   │  Testing and Validation   │
           │                   └──────────────────────────┘
           │                              │
           └──────────────◇───────────────┘
                          │
                          ▼
              ┌─────────────────────────┐       ┌──────────────────────────────┐
              │ Maintenance and Evaluation │─────│ Input: Implemented system.    │
              └─────────────────────────┘       │ Output: Maintained and        │
                          │                      │ updated system.               │
                          ▼                      └──────────────────────────────┘
          ┌──────────────────────────┐
          │ Periodic System Evaluation │
          └──────────────────────────┘
                          │
                          ▼
                          ◉
```

Definition of Information System Planning

Information system planning is a process carried out by an organization to determine the strategy and direction of using information technology to support operations and management objectives. According to McLeod, an information system is a system that has the ability to collect information from various sources and display that information with various media[28].

Tata Sutabri suggests that an information system is a system in an organization that meets the needs of daily transaction processing and supports managerial functions in strategic activities[29]. This means that information systems not only process data, but also play a role in strategic decision making that supports the achievement of organizational goals.

Erwan Arbie added that information systems must be able to provide accurate and timely information, which can be used by management and other stakeholders to make better decisions[30] . In this context, information systems become a vital tool to improve the efficiency and effectiveness of organizational operations.

---

[28] McLeod, R., & Schell, G. (2007). Management Information Systems. Fourth Edition.
[29] Sutabri, T. (2012). Management Information System. Andi Offset
[30] Arbie, E. (2015). Introduction to Information Systems. Gramedia.

According to Tafri D. Muhyuzir, information system planning includes a combination of people, facilities or technological tools, media, procedures, and controls aimed at organizing important communication networks and certain transaction processes. It also helps in providing the basis for proper decision making[31].

Kertahadi states that an information system is a tool for presenting useful information to its recipients. The goal is to provide information in planning, organizing, and operating a company[32]. Thus, information systems must be designed in such a way as to provide optimal benefits for all parts of the organization.

Good information system planning also pays attention to aspects of data security and protection, considering that the information managed is often sensitive and crucial to the organization's business continuity. Therefore, the integration of appropriate security protocols and access policies is an integral part of effective information system design and implementation.

---

[31] Muhyuzir, T. D. (2014). Information System Management. Elex Media Komputindo.

[32] Kertahadi, K. (2010). Information Systems in Management. Mitra Wacana Media.

Overall, good information system planning will help organizations achieve their strategic goals more effectively and efficiently. By understanding the need and purpose of information system planning, organizations can create an organized and unified structure, facilitating the smooth flow of information across organizational entities.

Example of Information System Planning at PT. INDOFOOD

Information system planning in companies like Indofood is an important step to support efficient and effective business operations. The following is an example of the steps in planning information systems in the Indofood company:

Identify Business Goals and Needs:

1. Start by identifying the Indofood company's business objectives. What do you want to achieve through the information system? For example, increased production efficiency, stock control, supply chain management, or improved customer service.

2. Business Process Identification: Identify the business processes that exist in an Indofood company. Make sure to understand how each process interacts with each other. For example, production, inventory management, distribution, and administration.

3. Identify User Needs: Determine who will use the information system (e.g., management, production operators, finance, etc.) and what they need from the system.

4. Evaluation of Available Technology: Review Indofood's existing technology and infrastructure. Consider whether the existing technology can be utilized or needs to be upgraded.

5. Design System Architecture: Design an information system architecture that will support the needs of the company. Decide whether to use a monolithic system or a distributed approach. Select the appropriate technology platform.

6. Identify Required Software: Choose software that suits the needs of the company. This could include ERP (Enterprise Resource Planning) software, supply chain management software, financial software, and so on.

7. Development and Implementation: After designing the system, do the system development and implementation. Make sure the system is well integrated with existing business processes.

8. Testing: Test the system thoroughly to ensure that all features and functionality are working properly. Also ensure that the system meets the user's needs.

9. User Training: Provide training to users so that they can operate the system properly.

10. Monitoring and Maintenance: Once the system is implemented, monitor it regularly and ensure that it continues to run well. Perform regular maintenance and repairs if needed.

11. Evaluation and Continuous Improvement: Conduct periodic evaluations of the system to ensure that the information system continues to meet the needs of the company. Improve or upgrade the system if there are changes in business needs.

12. Data Security and Protection: Ensure that Indofood's information systems have strong security measures in place to protect sensitive company data.

13. Project Management: Establish the appropriate project team, schedule, and budget to ensure that the planning and implementation of the system runs smoothly.

Information system planning at Indofood or any other company should always be tailored to the unique needs of the company and the market. It is important to continuously monitor and evaluate the system to keep it relevant and support the company's growth.

Example of Information System Planning at PT Dirgantara Yudha Artha

Asset management information system planning at PT Dirgantara Yudha Artha is a case study conducted in the asset management division. Here are some of the points obtained:

1. PT Dirgantara Yudha Artha needs an efficient asset management information system to support the activities of providing integrated information precisely and accurately, as well as supporting efficiency policies by providing paperless report information.

2. The asset management information system includes aspects of planning and implementation of budget submissions.

3. In the planning process, the author uses UML Tools to describe the system to be built.

4. The results of testing the budget planning and implementation information system at PT Dirgantara Indonesia show that this system can provide convenience in realizing, monitoring, and evaluating decision making and getting information quickly, precisely, and accurately about budget operations at the company.

In this context, asset management information system planning is important to support information provision activities and efficiency policies within PT Dirgantara Yudha Artha. The designed asset management information system enables the company to optimize the budget submission process and achieve efficiency policy goals.

CHAPTER 5: STRATEGIC PLANNING

Management information system (MIS) strategic planning is a critical process that helps organizations identify, develop, and implement information systems that support the company's goals and vision. The following are general steps in MIS strategic planning:

1. Identify the Vision and Goals of the Organization: Understand the organization's long-term vision and goals. Ensure that the MIS plan supports the achievement of these goals.

2. Identify Needs and Opportunities: Review the current and future information needs of the organization, Identify opportunities to improve efficiency, productivity and competitiveness through MIS.

3. Form a Planning Team: Form a team consisting of members from various departments who have an understanding of the organization's business needs and processes.

4. Review Current Conditions: Evaluate existing information systems, including technology infrastructure, applications and human resources involved in managing the MIS.

5. Strategic Plan Development, develop a MIS strategic plan that includes:

   a. The purpose and objectives of information systems.

   b. Technology development plan.

   c. Information security plan

   d. Data management plan.

   e. Human resource plan (training and development).

   f. Budget plan and financial resources.

6. Technology Evaluation: Review technologies that fit the needs of the organization. Consider appropriate hardware, software, platforms and cloud infrastructure.

7. Implementation Plan: Develop an implementation plan that includes the schedule, phasing, and monitoring of the MIS project. Ensure the necessary resources are available.

8. Change Management: Pay attention to effective change management, Communicate changes to employees and provide training if needed.

9. Evaluation and Monitoring: During and after implementation, conduct periodic evaluations to ensure the MIS is on track and contributing to the achievement of organizational goals.

10. Continuous Improvement: Make continuous improvements to the MIS in accordance with feedback, technological developments, and changes in business needs.

11. Information Security: Consider strict information security, including policies, procedures, encryption and security monitoring systems.

12. Performance Monitoring: Use performance metrics to monitor MIS performance and measure its impact on the organization.

Strategic planning of management information systems is an ongoing process that is adapted to changes in the business and technology environment. It helps organizations to leverage information technology in a way that supports their long-term goals and growth.

Strategic Planning Flowchart

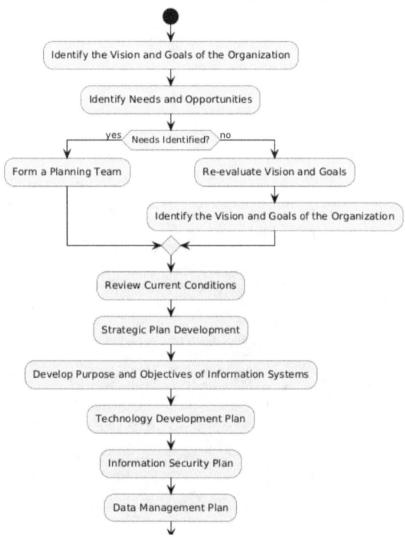

General Steps in MIS Strategic Planning

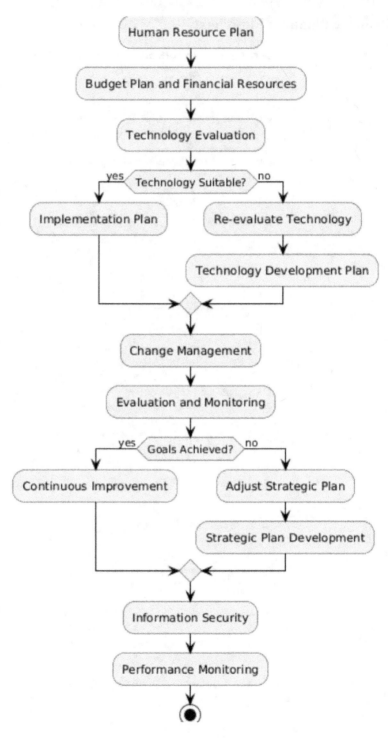

General Steps in MIS Strategic Planning:

1. Identify the Vision and Goals of the Organization: The process begins with understanding the long-term vision and specific goals of the organization. This step ensures that the MIS strategy aligns with the overall objectives of the organization.

2. Identify Needs and Opportunities: In this step, the organization identifies its current and future information needs and opportunities to improve efficiency, productivity, and competitiveness through MIS.

3. Decision Point - Needs Identified?: Here, a decision is made on whether the needs and opportunities have been adequately identified.

   a. If yes, proceed to form a planning team.

   b. If no, re-evaluate the vision and goals, then revisit the step to identify the vision and goals of the organization.

4. Form a Planning Team: A team comprising members from various departments is formed. This team has a comprehensive understanding of the business needs and processes of the organization.

5. Review Current Conditions: The existing information systems, technology infrastructure, applications, and human resources involved in managing the MIS are evaluated.

6. Strategic Plan Development: A strategic plan for MIS is developed. This includes multiple sub-steps:

a. Develop Purpose and Objectives of Information Systems: Define what the information system aims to achieve and its specific objectives.

b. Technology Development Plan: Outline the plan for technology development to support the MIS.

c. Information Security Plan: Develop a plan to ensure information security.

d. Data Management Plan: Plan how data will be managed and utilized.

e. Human Resource Plan: Plan for the training and development of human resources.

f. Budget Plan and Financial Resources: Plan the budget and allocate financial resources for the MIS.

7. Technology Evaluation: Evaluate the technologies identified in the strategic plan to ensure they meet the organization's needs.

8. Decision Point - Technology Suitable?: Decide if the evaluated technology is suitable.

a. If yes, proceed to implementation planning.

b. If no, re-evaluate the technology, then revisit the technology development plan.

9. Implementation Plan: Develop a detailed plan for implementing the MIS, including scheduling, resource allocation, and phasing.

10. Change Management: Implement change management practices to ensure smooth adoption of the new system. This

includes communicating changes and providing necessary training.

11. Evaluation and Monitoring: Regularly evaluate and monitor the MIS to ensure it is on track and contributing to achieving organizational goals.

12. Decision Point - Goals Achieved?: Determine if the goals set for the MIS have been achieved.

    a. If yes, continue with continuous improvement.

    b. If no, adjust the strategic plan, then revisit the strategic plan development step.

13. Continuous Improvement: Continuously improve the MIS based on feedback, technological advancements, and changing business needs.

14. Information Security: Ensure that strict information security measures are in place, including policies, procedures, encryption, and security monitoring systems.

15. Performance Monitoring: Use performance metrics to monitor the MIS and measure its impact on the organization.

This structured approach ensures that the MIS strategic planning process is thorough, aligns with organizational goals, and is continuously improved to meet evolving needs.

CHAPTER 6: INFORMATION SYSTEM DEVELOPMENT - SDLC

Information System Development with SDLC

Information system development is an important process in ensuring that information technology can support business operations effectively. One of the most commonly used approaches in information systems development is the System Development Life Cycle (SDLC). SDLC is a framework that helps development teams to plan, create, test, and implement information systems in a structured and efficient way[33].

1. Planning Stage

The first stage in the SDLC is planning. At this stage, business needs are identified, and the objectives of the new information system are formulated. A feasibility analysis is conducted to ensure that the project can be implemented within the constraints of time, cost, and available resources. Good planning helps avoid problems later on and ensures that all stakeholders have a clear understanding of the purpose and scope of the project[34].

---

[33] Laudon, K. C., & Laudon, J. P. (2018). Management Information Systems: Managing the Digital Firm (15th ed.). Pearson.

[34] McLeod, R., & Schell, G. (2007). Management Information Systems. Fourth Edition

2. Analysis Stage

After planning, the next stage is analysis. At this stage, user and business needs are analyzed in detail. The development team works closely with stakeholders to collect and document system requirements. This analysis involves creating business models and workflow diagrams to ensure that the developed system will meet the needs of the organization[35].

3. Design Stage

The design stage is the step where the system architecture and technical specifications are designed. At this stage, system designers create a more detailed model of the system, including the design of the database, user interface, and software components. This design should ensure that the system will be easy to use, efficient, and secure [36][37].

4. Development Stage

Once the design is complete, the development stage begins. In this stage, program code is written according to the design specifications. Developers work to turn the design into a system that can function.

---

[35] McLeod, R., & Schell, G. (2007). Management Information Systems. Fourth Edition

[36] Pressman, R. S. (2014). Software Engineering: A Practitioner's Approach (8th ed.). McGraw-Hill.

[37] ibid

This stage involves a lot of coding and programming, and the development team often uses the latest tools and technologies to ensure that the system runs smoothly[38].

5. Testing Phase

Testing is an important step to ensure that the system works as it should before it is implemented. At this stage, the system is thoroughly tested to find and fix bugs or errors. Testing includes unit testing, integration testing, system testing, and user acceptance testing. Good testing ensures that the developed system meets all requirements and is reliable in daily operation[39].

6. Implementation Stage

The implementation stage is when the tested system is deployed in the production environment. At this stage, data from the old system may need to be migrated to the new system, and users must be trained to use the new system. Successful implementation requires good planning and strong support from all parties involved[40].

---

[38] Pressman, R. S. (2014). Software Engineering: A Practitioner's Approach (8th ed.). McGraw-Hill.

[39] Laudon, K. C., & Laudon, J. P. (2018). Management Information Systems: Managing the Digital Firm (15th ed.). Pearson.

[40] McLeod, R., & Schell, G. (2007). Management Information Systems. Fourth Edition.

7. Maintenance Stage

Once the system is implemented, the maintenance stage begins. At this stage, the system is monitored and fixed if any issues arise. Maintenance also involves updating the system to improve performance or adding new features as per user requirements. Ongoing maintenance ensures that the system remains effective and relevant in supporting business operations[41].

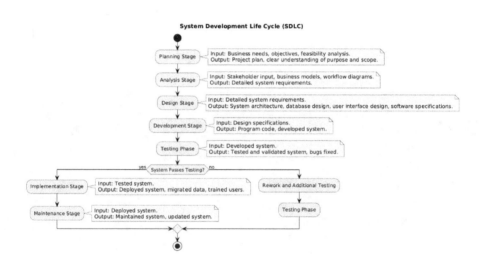

[41] Pressman, R. S. (2014). Software Engineering: A Practitioner's Approach (8th ed.). McGraw-Hill.

Information system development using the SDLC approach is a structured and systematic process. By following the stages of the SDLC, organizations can ensure that the information systems developed meet business needs, are efficient and reliable. This approach also helps identify and address problems before they become major obstacles, ensuring successful implementation and effective maintenance [42] [43] [44].

[42] Laudon, K. C., & Laudon, J. P. (2018). Management Information Systems: Managing the Digital Firm (15th ed.). Pearson.

[43] McLeod, R., & Schell, G. (2007). Management Information Systems. Fourth Edition.

[44] Pressman, R. S. (2014). Software Engineering: A Practitioner's Approach (8th ed.). McGraw-Hill.

Chapter 7: Management Information System Implementation

According to Wheny Khristianto, Totok Supriyanto, and Sri Wahyuni, Management Information System (MIS) is a key component in the operation of an organization. It is a system designed to meet the diverse needs of information management in an organization. MIS is not just a technological tool, but also serves as a link between various important elements in the organization, including daily transaction processing, operational support, managerial, and strategic planning. In addition, it also plays an important role in providing information needed by external parties related to the organization, such as shareholders, government, and other stakeholders[45] .

In the ever-changing business era, MIS has become one of the fastest growing fields of study. This is in line with the rapid development of the business world and the continuous advancement of information technology. Organizations must be able to deal with rapid changes in their business environment, and MIS is a very important tool in addressing this challenge. It enables organizations to manage, integrate, and optimize various aspects of their business more efficiently and effectively.

---

[45]https://www.academia.edu/40111374/Buku_Ajar_SISTEM_INFORMA SI_MANAJEMEN

In this increasingly connected world, MIS is becoming an essential cornerstone in making accurate decisions and managing an organization's day-to-day operations.

The Management Information System (Sociotechnical Approach) textbook written by Wheny Khristianto, Totok Supriyanto, and Sri Wahyuni is an invaluable resource in understanding MIS in depth. The book presents a comprehensive overview of various aspects of MIS, including basic concepts, components, information processing, needs analysis, and management information system development. By referring to this book, practitioners and students can gain a deeper understanding of how MIS contributes to the success of an organization. This book is a very useful reference in understanding MIS as a tool that supports the management of information and data in an organization [46][47].

Management Information Systems is not just about technology or software. It is a concept that encompasses various aspects, including operational management, data analysis, and strategic decision-making. MIS helps organizations to incorporate these various elements into their daily operations.

---

[46]Mufidah, Zahrotul. (2017). APPLICATION OF INFORMATION SYSTEM STRATEGIC MATRIX: Case Study at the Public Library and Regional Archives Office (DPAD) of Malang City. BIBLIOTIKA: Journal of Library and Information Studies. 1. 10.17977/um008v1i12017p058.

[47]https://www.studocu.com/id/document/universitas-mulawarman/komput er

Thus, MIS is a tool that enables organizations to achieve their goals better and more efficiently[48].

Information processing is a key element in a driver's license. It enables organizations to collect, manage, and analyze relevant information for various aspects of their business. By generating efficient information, organizations can make better decisions, optimize their operations, and respond more quickly to market changes. It also helps organizations to identify new business opportunities and better manage risks. With strong information delivery capabilities, MIS becomes an essential tool in optimizing organizational performance.

Needs analysis is a crucial first step in the development of a driver's license. Organizations need to clearly understand what they need from their information system. This involves identifying the problems to be solved, the opportunities to be exploited, and the business requirements to be met. A careful needs analysis will help organizations design and develop an information system that suits their needs. In other words, the MIS will be built to address challenges and opportunities that are specific to an organization[49].

---

[48]https://www.academia.edu/40111374/Buku_Ajar_SISTEM_INFORMA SI_MANAJEMEN

[49]Khristianto, W., Supriyanto, T., & Wahyuni, S. (2015). Management Information System (Sociotechnical Approach).

Management information system development is the next step after needs analysis. This development process includes the selection of appropriate technology, database design, application development, and user training. In this process, organizations will design and implement information systems that suit their business needs. With effective information systems, organizations can improve their operations, optimize business processes, and better achieve their business goals.

In the ever-changing world of business, effective management information is critical. It is a critical tool in supporting accurate decision-making, managing day-to-day operations, and planning business strategies. With a solid understanding of MIS, organizations can plan and implement information systems that support their business goals and needs. MIS helps organizations to integrate human resources, technology, and business processes in order to achieve set business goals. Therefore, a strong understanding of MIS is an important first step in starting a business and running it successfully.

In the ever-evolving digital age, the use of information technology to support business operations is becoming increasingly important. MIS helps organizations to integrate information technology into their daily operations and make it an effective tool in achieving business goals.

Through careful information transmission and accurate data analysis, MIS helps organizations to improve efficiency, optimize operations, and better achieve their goals. Therefore, an understanding of MIS is an important first step in starting a business.

Management Information System Implementation

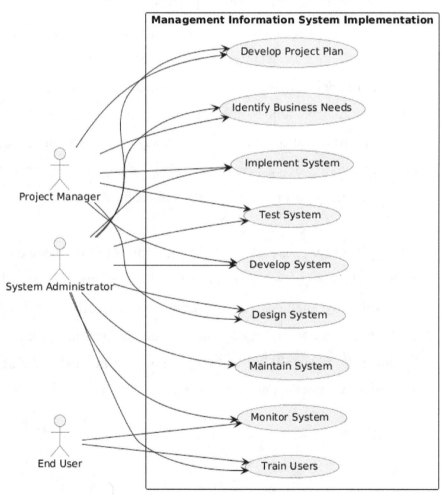

CHAPTER 8: SECURITY AND PRIVACY IN INFORMATION SYSTEMS

In the increasingly advanced digital era, security and privacy in information systems are crucial for the sustainability of an organization's operations and reputation. Information is a highly valuable asset, including customer data, financial information, and corporate secrets. Protecting this information is not only essential to prevent financial losses but also to maintain stakeholder trust and comply with applicable regulations[50]. Threats to information security can come from various sources, including hackers seeking financial gain, malware that can damage or steal data, and human errors, which are often the primary cause of information leaks[51].

Organizations need to implement various methods and technologies to protect their information. Encryption is one of the most effective methods for protecting data by converting it into a code that cannot be read without the proper decryption key. Additionally, firewalls act as barriers between internal and external networks, preventing unauthorized access.

---

[50] Pfleeger, C. P., Pfleeger, S. L., & Margulies, J. (2015). Security in Computing (5th ed.). Prentice Hall.
[51] Bishop, M. (2018). Computer Security: Art and Science (2nd ed.). Addison-Wesley.

Intrusion detection systems monitor network activity to detect and respond to suspicious activities. Furthermore, access controls ensure that only authorized users can access certain information[52].

This chapter will delve deeply into the basic concepts of information security, the various threats faced, the methods and technologies used to protect information, privacy policies and related regulations, as well as case studies of information security breaches that provide valuable lessons. Understanding and implementing appropriate information security measures is key to maintaining integrity and trust in this complex digital world.

Basic Concepts of Information Security

Information security is the practice of protecting information from various threats to ensure business continuity, minimize risk, and maximize opportunities and return on investment. In today's digital era, information is one of the most important assets for organizations.

---

[52] Stallings, W., & Brown, L. (2018). Computer Security: Principles and Practice. Pearson Education.

The basic concepts of information security include three main principles: confidentiality, integrity, and availability.

Confidentiality ensures that information is only accessible to authorized parties. Integrity guarantees that information remains accurate and unchanged without permission. Availability ensures that information is always accessible to users who need it[53].

Threats to Information Security

Threats to information security come from various sources and can be either internal or external. Internal threats may originate from dissatisfied or negligent employees, while external threats can come from hackers, malware, and other cyber attacks. These threats can lead to data theft, system damage, and business operation disruptions. The increased use of digital technology also expands the attack surface, raising the risk and complexity of threats[54].

Threats to information security come from various sources and can be either internal or external. Internal threats may originate from dissatisfied or negligent employees, while external threats can come from hackers, malware, and other cyber attacks. These threats can lead to data theft, system damage, and business operation disruptions.

---

[53] Whitman, M. E., & Mattord, H. J. (2022). Principles of Information Security. Cengage Learning.
[54] Anderson, R., & Moore, T. (2006). The Economics of Information Security. Science, 314(5799), 610-613.

The increased use of digital technology also expands the attack surface, raising the risk and complexity of threats.

Internal threats can be particularly insidious, as they often involve individuals who already have some level of access to the organization's systems and data. This can include employees who are disgruntled or seeking personal gain, as well as those who unintentionally compromise security through careless actions, such as falling for phishing scams or failing to follow security protocols.

External threats, on the other hand, encompass a wide range of malicious activities. Hackers may attempt to infiltrate networks to steal sensitive information, disrupt services, or hold data for ransom. Malware, including viruses, worms, and ransomware, can infect systems and cause widespread damage. Cyber attacks can also involve sophisticated techniques such as social engineering, where attackers manipulate individuals into divulging confidential information.

The growing prevalence of Internet of Things (IoT) devices, cloud computing, and mobile technologies has further exacerbated the security landscape. Each new device and platform introduces potential vulnerabilities that attackers can exploit. Organizations must contend with securing a diverse array of technologies, often with limited resources and expertise.

To effectively combat these threats, a comprehensive approach to information security is essential. This includes implementing robust technical controls, such as firewalls, intrusion detection systems, and encryption. Additionally, organizations must establish strong policies and procedures, conduct regular security training and awareness programs for employees, and perform ongoing risk assessments and security audits.

Moreover, staying updated with the latest security trends and threat intelligence is crucial. Collaboration with industry peers and participation in information-sharing communities can help organizations stay ahead of emerging threats and adopt best practices. By adopting a proactive and multi-layered defense strategy, organizations can better protect their information assets and ensure resilience against the ever-evolving landscape of information security threats.

Methods and Technologies to Protect Information

Various methods and technologies are used to protect information. These include encryption, firewalls, intrusion detection systems, and access controls. Encryption converts data into a format that cannot be read without the proper decryption key, while firewalls act as barriers between internal and external networks.

Intrusion detection systems monitor networks for suspicious activity, and access controls ensure that only authorized users can access certain information. Implementing physical security, such as surveillance and restricted access to facilities, is also important in protecting information[55].

Various methods and technologies are used to protect information. These include encryption, firewalls, intrusion detection systems, and access controls. Encryption converts data into a format that cannot be read without the proper decryption key, while firewalls act as barriers between internal and external networks. Intrusion detection systems monitor networks for suspicious activity, and access controls ensure that only authorized users can access certain information. Implementing physical security, such as surveillance and restricted access to facilities, is also important in protecting information.

---

[55] Stallings, W., & Brown, L. (2018). Computer Security: Principles and Practice. Pearson Education.

In addition to these measures, organizations often employ advanced technologies such as multi-factor authentication (MFA), which adds an extra layer of security by requiring users to provide multiple forms of identification before gaining access to sensitive data. Data loss prevention (DLP) tools are also widely used to monitor and control data transfers, ensuring that sensitive information does not leave the organization unauthorized.

Network segmentation is another crucial practice, dividing a network into smaller, isolated segments to contain potential breaches and limit the movement of malicious actors within the system. Endpoint security solutions, including antivirus and anti-malware software, protect individual devices from threats and ensure that only secure and compliant devices can connect to the network.

Regular security assessments and audits help identify vulnerabilities and ensure compliance with security policies and regulations. Penetration testing, or ethical hacking, is a proactive approach where security professionals simulate attacks to uncover weaknesses before malicious actors can exploit them.

Furthermore, establishing a robust incident response plan is vital for promptly addressing and mitigating the impact of security breaches. This plan should include predefined procedures for detecting, investigating, and responding to incidents, as well as communication protocols to keep stakeholders informed.

Security awareness training for employees is equally important, as human error is often a significant factor in security incidents. Educating staff on recognizing phishing attempts, following best practices for password management, and understanding the importance of data protection can significantly reduce the risk of breaches.

Finally, organizations should stay informed about the latest security threats and trends by participating in information-sharing initiatives and collaborating with industry peers. By leveraging threat intelligence and adopting a multi-layered defense strategy, organizations can better safeguard their information assets and maintain resilience in the face of evolving cyber threats.

Privacy Policies and Related Regulations

Privacy policies and related regulations play a crucial role in protecting personal information and sensitive data. Laws such as the General Data Protection Regulation (GDPR) in Europe and the Health Insurance Portability and Accountability Act (HIPAA) in the United States set standards for handling personal data. Organizations must comply with these regulations to avoid legal penalties and maintain their reputation. Internal privacy policies should also be developed to ensure that employee and customer data is protected in accordance with applicable regulations[56].

---

[56] Solove, D. J., & Schwartz, P. M. (2020). Information Privacy Law. Aspen Publishers.

Privacy policies and related regulations play a crucial role in protecting personal information and sensitive data. Laws such as the General Data Protection Regulation (GDPR) in Europe and the Health Insurance Portability and Accountability Act (HIPAA) in the United States set standards for handling personal data. Organizations must comply with these regulations to avoid legal penalties and maintain their reputation. Internal privacy policies should also be developed to ensure that employee and customer data is protected in accordance with applicable regulations.

Effective privacy policies outline how personal data is collected, stored, processed, and shared, ensuring transparency and accountability. These policies should detail the types of data collected, the purposes for which the data is used, and the measures taken to protect the data from unauthorized access or breaches. Organizations should also define the rights of individuals regarding their personal data, including the right to access, correct, or delete their information.

Regular training and awareness programs for employees are essential to ensure that everyone understands their responsibilities in protecting personal data. Employees should be educated on the importance of privacy, the specific requirements of relevant regulations, and the organization's internal policies. This helps to create a culture of privacy within the organization and reduces the risk of data breaches caused by human error.

Data protection officers (DPOs) or privacy officers should be appointed to oversee the organization's compliance with privacy regulations and internal policies. These officers are responsible for monitoring data protection practices, conducting regular audits, and serving as the point of contact for data protection authorities and individuals whose data is being processed.

Organizations should also implement technical and organizational measures to protect personal data. This includes data encryption, access controls, regular security assessments, and incident response plans. Ensuring data minimization, where only the necessary amount of data is collected and retained, can also reduce the risk of exposure.

Privacy impact assessments (PIAs) should be conducted for new projects or systems that involve the processing of personal data. These assessments help identify and mitigate potential privacy risks, ensuring that privacy is considered from the outset.

In addition to complying with regulations, organizations should be proactive in adapting to changes in the regulatory landscape. This involves staying informed about new and emerging privacy laws and adjusting policies and practices accordingly. Participation in industry groups and information-sharing initiatives can provide valuable insights and best practices for managing privacy effectively.

By adhering to privacy policies and regulations, organizations not only protect sensitive data but also build trust with customers and stakeholders. Demonstrating a commitment to privacy can enhance an organization's reputation, foster customer loyalty, and provide a competitive advantage in today's data-driven world.

Case Studies of Information Security Breaches and Lessons Learned

In 2017, Equifax, one of the three major credit bureaus in the United States, experienced a massive security breach that resulted in the theft of personal data of approximately 147 million people. The stolen data included names, Social Security numbers, birth dates, addresses, and, in some cases, driver's license numbers and credit card information[57].

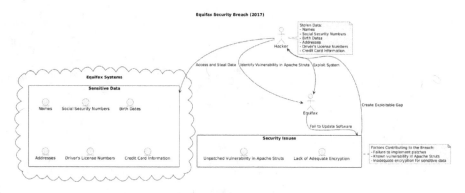

---

[57] Fruhlinger, J. (2020). Equifax Data Breach FAQ: What Happened, Who Was Affected, What Was the Impact? CSO Online.

The Equifax hack occurred due to several weaknesses in the company's security system. One of the main factors was the failure to update the Apache Struts software, which had a known vulnerability. Although a patch for this vulnerability had been released several months before the breach, Equifax did not implement it promptly. This gap allowed hackers to exploit the system and access sensitive data[58].

Additionally, the lack of adequate encryption for sensitive data also contributed to the severity of the breach. While some data was encrypted, much of it was not well-protected, making it easier for hackers to access.

---

[58] Perlroth, IN. (2021). This Is How They Tell Me the World Ends: The Cyber-Weapons Arms Race. Bloomsbury Publishing.

The lack of effective security oversight and management further exacerbated the situation, as signs of the breach were not detected in a timely manner.

Preventing Future Security Breaches

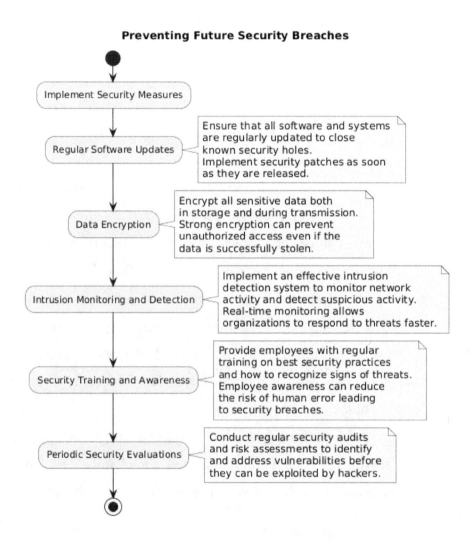

To prevent similar events in the future, several steps and solutions can be implemented:

- Regular Software Updates: Organizations must ensure that all software and systems are regularly updated to close known security holes. This includes implementing security patches as soon as they are released.

- Data Encryption: All sensitive data should be encrypted both in storage and during transmission. Strong encryption can prevent unauthorized access even if the data is successfully stolen.[59].

- Intrusion Monitoring and Detection: An effective intrusion detection system should be implemented to monitor network activity and detect suspicious activity. Real-time monitoring allows organizations to respond to threats faster.[60].

- Security Training and Awareness: Employees should be provided with regular training on best security practices and how to recognize signs of threats. Employee awareness can reduce the risk of human error that can lead to security breaches[61].

- Periodic Security Evaluations: Regular security audits and risk assessments should be conducted to identify and address vulnerabilities before they can be exploited by hackers.[62].

---

[59] Stallings, W., & Brown, L. (2018). Computer Security: Principles and Practice. Pearson Education.
[60] Scarfone, K., & Mell, P. (2007). Guide to Intrusion Detection and Prevention Systems (IDPS). NIST Special Publication 800-94.
[61] Whitman, M. E., & Mattord, H. J. (2022). Principles of Information Security. Cengage Learning.
[62] Hinson, G. (2018). Security Risk Assessment: Managing and

The Equifax hack provides an important lesson about the importance of proactive and comprehensive security management in protecting sensitive data. By implementing the right preventive measures, organizations can reduce the risk of security breaches and protect their customers' personal data.

_____

Conducting. CRC Press.

CHAPTER 9: FUTURE DIRECTIONS AND EMERGING TRENDS IN MANAGEMENT INFORMATION SYSTEMS

As we move further into the digital age, the landscape of Management Information Systems (MIS) continues to evolve rapidly. Emerging technologies and trends are reshaping how organizations leverage information systems to achieve their strategic goals. This chapter explores the future directions and emerging trends in MIS, providing insights into the innovations that are set to transform the field.

One of the most significant trends is the integration of artificial intelligence (AI) and machine learning (ML) into MIS. These technologies are enabling more sophisticated data analysis, predictive modeling, and automation of routine tasks. AI-driven systems can provide deeper insights into customer behavior, optimize supply chain operations, and enhance decision-making processes. As AI and ML continue to advance, their applications within MIS are expected to expand, driving efficiencies and uncovering new opportunities for organizations.

The rise of big data analytics is another key trend. The ability to process and analyze vast amounts of data in real-time is empowering organizations to make more informed decisions. Big data analytics helps businesses understand market trends, identify potential risks, and tailor products and services to meet customer needs. With the increasing volume of data generated daily, the role of big data in MIS will only become more critical.

Cybersecurity remains a top priority as the number of cyber threats continues to grow. Future MIS must incorporate robust security measures to protect sensitive information from breaches and attacks. This includes the use of advanced encryption, multi-factor authentication, and continuous monitoring of network activities. As cyber threats evolve, so too must the security protocols within MIS to safeguard organizational data.

Cloud computing is revolutionizing how information systems are deployed and managed. The flexibility and scalability offered by cloud solutions allow organizations to access and store data more efficiently. Cloud-based MIS can be easily updated and scaled according to business needs, reducing the reliance on physical infrastructure. This trend is expected to continue, with more organizations adopting cloud technologies to enhance their MIS capabilities.

The Internet of Things (IoT) is also making a significant impact on MIS. IoT devices generate vast amounts of data that can be harnessed to improve operational efficiency, monitor systems in real-time, and create more responsive environments. The integration of IoT with MIS enables better asset management, predictive maintenance, and enhanced customer experiences.

Blockchain technology, known for its security and transparency, is emerging as a powerful tool for MIS. Its applications in securing transactions, verifying identities, and managing supply chains are being explored across various industries. The decentralized nature of blockchain can enhance data integrity and trust within MIS, providing a secure framework for digital interactions.

In summary, the future of Management Information Systems is poised for exciting advancements driven by AI, big data, cybersecurity, cloud computing, IoT, and blockchain. Organizations must stay abreast of these trends to leverage MIS effectively and maintain a competitive edge in the rapidly changing digital landscape.

Summary and Conclusion

This book has delved into the comprehensive world of Management Information Systems (MIS), exploring its various facets and applications in modern organizations. We began with an overview of marketing and manufacturing information systems, highlighting their critical roles in business operations. The discussion then moved to HR and accounting information systems, emphasizing their importance in managing human resources and financial data.

We examined the significance of financial information systems and the intricacies of information system design, planning, and implementation. The strategic planning and development of information systems using the System Development Life Cycle (SDLC) were detailed, providing a structured approach to system development.

The implementation of MIS was thoroughly discussed, including the challenges and best practices for successful deployment. Security and privacy in information systems were emphasized, underscoring the need for robust protection measures in the digital age.

In the closing chapter, we looked towards the future, identifying emerging trends and technologies that will shape the evolution of MIS. The integration of AI, big data, cybersecurity, cloud computing, IoT, and blockchain were highlighted as key drivers of future advancements in MIS.

In conclusion, Management Information Systems are indispensable tools that enable organizations to operate efficiently, make informed decisions, and stay competitive in a rapidly evolving digital world. By understanding and leveraging the principles and technologies discussed in this book, organizations can harness the full potential of MIS to drive growth and innovation.

Chapter 10: Artificial Intelligence and Big Data in Management Information Systems

Introduction to AI and Big Data in Management Information Systems

Definition and Basic Concepts of Artificial Intelligence (AI) and Big Data

Artificial Intelligence (AI) and Big Data are two transformative technologies that have redefined the way organizations operate, process information, and make decisions. AI is a branch of computer science that enables machines to mimic human cognitive functions such as learning, reasoning, and decision-making (Russell & Norvig, 2021). It comprises various subfields, including machine learning (ML), natural language processing (NLP), deep learning, and robotics, which empower systems to analyze data, recognize patterns, and automate tasks.

Big Data, on the other hand, refers to massive and complex datasets that traditional data-processing tools cannot efficiently handle. Big Data is characterized by the **5Vs**:

1. **Volume** – The sheer amount of data generated from digital interactions, IoT devices, social media, and business transactions.
2. **Velocity** – The speed at which data is created, transferred, and processed in real-time.
3. **Variety** – The diverse formats of data, including structured

(databases), semi-structured (XML, JSON), and unstructured (videos, images, text).

4. **Veracity** – The quality and reliability of data, ensuring accuracy for effective decision-making.

5. **Value** – The potential insights derived from data that help businesses drive growth and innovation.

The integration of AI and Big Data has transformed Management Information Systems (MIS) by enabling organizations to move beyond traditional data reporting to predictive and prescriptive analytics. By leveraging AI-driven algorithms, businesses can forecast trends, optimize processes, and personalize customer experiences (Brynjolfsson & McAfee, 2017).

Case Studies: AI and Big Data in Real-World Applications

1. AI-Powered Customer Experience: Netflix's Recommendation Engine

Challenge:
Netflix needed a way to retain customers and improve content discovery amid a growing library of digital content.

Solution:
Netflix implemented an **AI-driven recommendation system** that uses **machine learning algorithms** to analyze viewing history, user preferences, and engagement patterns. The system personalizes movie and TV show suggestions, resulting in **80% of content**

watched on Netflix being driven by recommendations (Gomez-Uribe & Hunt, 2016).

Impact:

- Increased customer retention rates and user engagement.
- Enhanced content discovery, reducing churn rates and improving subscription renewals.

2. *Big Data and Predictive Analytics: Walmart's Demand Forecasting*

Challenge:

Walmart, as one of the world's largest retailers, faced challenges in inventory management and supply chain optimization.

Solution:

Walmart deployed a **Big Data analytics system** that collects **petabytes of sales data**, weather patterns, and economic indicators to predict product demand. AI models analyze this data to optimize stock levels and prevent overstocking or understocking (Davenport, 2018).

Impact:

- Reduction in **inventory waste and supply chain inefficiencies**.
- Increased revenue by ensuring the right products are available at the right time.

3. AI in Healthcare: IBM Watson in Cancer Diagnosis

Challenge:

Doctors face difficulties in analyzing vast amounts of patient data and medical literature to make precise diagnoses.

Solution:

IBM Watson, a cognitive AI system, processes medical literature and patient data to assist doctors in diagnosing **complex diseases such as cancer**. By leveraging **natural language processing (NLP)**, Watson provides evidence-based treatment recommendations.

Impact:

- **30% improvement** in diagnostic accuracy in certain cancer types.
- Reduction in diagnosis time, allowing doctors to focus on patient care.

The Future of AI and Big Data in Management Information Systems

Looking ahead, AI and Big Data will continue to shape the landscape of Management Information Systems. Some key areas of development include:

1. **AI-Driven Business Intelligence (BI)**
   - Businesses will shift towards **augmented analytics**, where AI automates data visualization and insights generation.

2. **Autonomous Decision-Making Systems**
   - AI-powered systems will provide **real-time business insights** with minimal human intervention.

3. **Edge AI and Real-Time Data Processing**
   - Edge computing and AI will enable **faster processing of data directly on IoT devices**, reducing latency and enhancing efficiency.

4. **Enhanced Cybersecurity with AI**
   - AI-driven cybersecurity systems will detect and mitigate threats in real-time using anomaly detection techniques.

The integration of AI and Big Data into Management Information Systems represents a paradigm shift in how organizations operate and make decisions. By leveraging AI-driven automation, predictive analytics, and real-time decision intelligence, businesses can achieve higher efficiency, improved customer experiences, and enhanced competitiveness in the digital economy. As AI technology continues to evolve, ethical considerations and regulatory compliance will play a crucial role in ensuring responsible AI adoption.

The Role of AI in Management Information Systems

Artificial Intelligence (AI) is revolutionizing Management Information Systems (MIS) by enabling automation, predictive analytics, and intelligent decision-making. AI enhances business operations by streamlining workflows, reducing human errors, improving efficiency, and facilitating data-driven strategies. This section explores the key roles of AI in MIS, focusing on business process automation, machine learning, and AI applications in HR, marketing, and finance.

---

1. Business Process Automation and Decision-Making

AI-driven automation has transformed traditional business processes, eliminating manual tasks and enhancing real-time decision-making. By integrating AI into MIS workflows, organizations can achieve:

a. Process Optimization with Robotic Process Automation (RPA)

- **RPA uses AI-powered bots** to automate repetitive administrative tasks such as **data entry, invoice processing, and customer service requests** (Aguirre & Rodriguez, 2017).
- Example: **Banking institutions** utilize **AI chatbots** to process transactions, answer customer queries, and detect fraudulent activities, reducing workload and improving efficiency.

b. Intelligent Decision Support Systems (IDSS)

- AI-powered **decision support systems** analyze **historical and real-time data** to provide managers with **predictive**

insights for strategic planning.

- Example: **AI-based fraud detection systems** in banks analyze transactional behavior to identify anomalies and prevent financial losses.

c. AI in Supply Chain and Logistics

- AI enables **predictive supply chain management**, optimizing inventory levels, forecasting demand, and reducing operational bottlenecks.
- Example: **Amazon's AI-driven logistics system** predicts product demand, automates warehouse management, and optimizes last-mile delivery routes.

By automating business operations, AI minimizes human intervention, enhances efficiency, accuracy, and cost-effectiveness, and allows organizations to focus on innovation and strategic growth.

2. Machine Learning and Predictive Analytics in Management Information Systems

Machine learning (ML), a subset of AI, enables MIS to learn from data patterns and improve decision-making without explicit programming. Businesses leverage ML-powered predictive analytics to forecast trends, assess risks, and optimize strategies.

a. Predictive Analytics for Business Strategy

- ML algorithms analyze large datasets to **identify market trends, predict consumer behavior, and optimize business performance**.
- Example: **Retail companies like Walmart** use ML-powered predictive analytics to adjust pricing strategies and optimize product placement based on consumer purchasing patterns.

b. AI-Powered Risk Management and Fraud Detection

- AI analyzes transactional data to detect **fraudulent activities, credit risks, and cyber threats** in real time.
- Example: **Financial institutions use AI-driven anomaly detection models** to flag unusual transactions and prevent cyber fraud.

c. AI-Driven Sentiment Analysis in Decision Making

- Natural Language Processing (NLP) enables AI to **analyze customer feedback, social media interactions, and reviews** to gauge customer sentiment.
- Example: **E-commerce platforms like Amazon and eBay** leverage AI sentiment analysis to **personalize product recommendations and improve customer experiences**.

Machine learning in MIS **enhances data-driven decision-making**, allowing organizations to make informed choices that **boost profitability, optimize resources, and enhance operational efficiency**.

3. AI in Human Resource Management, Marketing, and Finance

AI has become an integral part of HR, marketing, and finance, transforming recruitment, employee engagement, customer targeting, and financial analysis.

a. AI in Human Resource Management (HRM)

AI improves HR operations by **automating recruitment, talent management, and employee engagement**.

- **Automated Resume Screening:**
  - AI-powered **Applicant Tracking Systems (ATS)** screen resumes, match candidates with job descriptions, and reduce hiring time.
  - Example: **LinkedIn's AI-driven hiring tool** analyzes professional profiles to recommend suitable candidates to recruiters.
- **Employee Performance and Engagement Analytics:**
  - AI-based HR analytics track **employee productivity, well-being, and satisfaction** using predictive modeling.
  - Example: **AI-driven employee engagement platforms** like **Peakon** analyze survey responses to identify workplace trends and recommend interventions.
- **AI in Employee Training and Career Development:**
  - AI-powered learning platforms personalize **training**

programs based on employee skill gaps and career aspirations.

- ○ Example: **IBM Watson's AI-based HR system** recommends professional development courses tailored to employee competencies.

AI in HR **enhances workforce management, reduces recruitment bias, and improves overall employee productivity**.

b. AI in Marketing: Personalized Customer Experiences

AI-driven marketing enables businesses to **target the right customers, optimize campaigns, and enhance brand engagement**.

- **AI-Powered Personalization:**
  - ○ AI analyzes **customer behavior, preferences, and browsing history** to deliver personalized marketing content.
  - ○ Example: **Netflix's recommendation engine** suggests content based on user viewing habits, increasing engagement and retention rates.
- **Chatbots and Conversational AI:**
  - ○ AI-powered **chatbots handle customer queries, process orders, and provide real-time support**.
  - ○ Example: **Sephora's AI-driven chatbot** offers **personalized beauty recommendations** based on customer preferences.
- **AI in Digital Advertising:**

- AI optimizes **ad placements, budgets, and content based on predictive analytics**.
- Example: **Google Ads and Facebook Ads** use AI to target ads to **users based on demographics, interests, and behavior**.

By **leveraging AI-powered marketing strategies**, businesses can improve **customer engagement, boost sales, and enhance brand loyalty**.

c. AI in Financial Management: Fraud Detection and Predictive Analytics

AI enhances **financial planning, fraud prevention, and investment strategies**.

- **AI in Fraud Detection:**
  - AI-powered **fraud detection models analyze transactional patterns** to detect anomalies.
  - Example: **Mastercard and Visa use AI to flag suspicious transactions**, reducing fraud-related losses.
- **AI in Financial Forecasting:**
  - Predictive analytics models analyze **market trends, stock performance, and economic indicators** to guide investment decisions.
  - Example: **Hedge funds and trading firms use AI-based algorithms** to execute high-frequency

trades and predict stock price movements.

- **Automated Financial Reporting:**
  - ○ AI automates **financial data collection, auditing, and compliance monitoring**.
  - ○ Example: **JP Morgan's COiN (Contract Intelligence) platform** uses AI to review legal documents, reducing contract analysis time from **360,000 hours to seconds**.

AI-driven finance systems **enhance efficiency, minimize risks, and provide strategic insights for decision-making**.

AI has become a critical driver of digital transformation in Management Information Systems. By automating business processes, enhancing predictive analytics, and transforming HR, marketing, and finance, AI empowers organizations to make data-driven decisions, optimize resources, and improve customer experiences. Looking forward, the **integration of AI with emerging technologies** such as **Blockchain, Edge Computing, and Quantum AI** will **further enhance MIS capabilities**, enabling businesses to operate with **greater efficiency, agility, and intelligence**.

Big Data and Its Application in Organizations

Big Data has revolutionized how organizations operate, analyze information, and make strategic decisions. By leveraging massive datasets, businesses can extract valuable insights, improve efficiency, and gain a competitive advantage. This section explores the fundamental concepts of Big Data, its role in business optimization, and data management approaches using Data Warehousing and Data Lakes.

1. The Fundamental Concepts of Big Data: Volume, Variety, Velocity, and Veracity

Big Data is characterized by four core dimensions, commonly known as the 4Vs (McKinsey Global Institute, 2011):

a. Volume – The Scale of Data

- The sheer amount of data generated from various sources, including **customer interactions, IoT sensors, social media, financial transactions, and enterprise systems**.
- Example: **Facebook processes over 4 petabytes of data daily**, including user posts, photos, and videos.

b. Variety – Different Data Types

- Big Data consists of **structured, semi-structured, and unstructured data** from multiple sources.
    - **Structured Data:** Databases, spreadsheets, and transactional data.
    - **Semi-Structured Data:** JSON, XML files, and email records.
    - **Unstructured Data:** Videos, images, social media posts, and website logs.
- Example: **Amazon combines transactional data, customer**

reviews, and browsing behavior to personalize product recommendations.

c. Velocity – The Speed of Data Processing

- Data is generated and processed **in real-time or near real-time**, requiring **fast analytics and decision-making**.
- Example: **Stock exchanges like NASDAQ analyze millions of transactions per second to detect trends and execute trades instantly**.

d. Veracity – The Reliability of Data

- Ensuring data accuracy, consistency, and quality is crucial for **effective decision-making**.
- Example: **Healthcare organizations use AI to clean and validate patient data before making diagnostic recommendations**.

Big Data's 4Vs define how businesses capture, process, and extract meaningful insights to drive innovation and operational excellence.

2. The Role of Big Data in Business Optimization

Big Data enables organizations to optimize operations, enhance customer experiences, and improve decision-making through data-driven insights.

a. Customer Behavior Analysis and Personalization

- Businesses analyze consumer behavior, purchase history, and preferences to **deliver personalized recommendations and targeted marketing**.
- Example: **Netflix uses machine learning to analyze viewer preferences and suggest content based on past interactions**.

b. Operational Efficiency and Cost Reduction

- Big Data analytics helps **identify inefficiencies, reduce waste, and optimize resource allocation**.
- Example: **General Electric (GE) uses IoT and predictive analytics to reduce machinery downtime and optimize maintenance schedules**.

c. Fraud Detection and Risk Management

- Financial institutions use **Big Data analytics to detect fraudulent transactions and assess credit risks**.
- Example: **Banks like JPMorgan Chase leverage AI and Big Data to analyze transaction patterns and prevent cyber fraud**.

d. Supply Chain and Logistics Optimization

- Companies use **real-time analytics to optimize inventory, reduce transportation costs, and enhance delivery speed**.
- Example: **Walmart's Big Data system predicts demand fluctuations and adjusts inventory levels accordingly**.

By leveraging Big Data, organizations can make smarter decisions, improve efficiency, and enhance competitiveness in a dynamic business landscape.

3. Data Management in Organizations: Data Warehousing and Data Lakes

Effective Big Data management requires efficient storage, retrieval, and analysis. Organizations use two primary approaches: Data Warehousing and Data Lakes.

a. Data Warehousing: Structured Data Storage for Business Intelligence

A **Data Warehouse** is a centralized repository that stores **structured and processed data** for business analytics and reporting (Kimball & Ross, 2013).

- **Key Characteristics:**
  - Stores **structured, cleansed, and pre-processed data**.
  - Optimized for **querying, reporting, and historical analysis**.
  - Uses **schema-on-write**, meaning data must be structured before being stored.
- **Use Case Example:**
  - **Retail Industry:** Walmart uses a **Data Warehouse** to consolidate global sales data, allowing executives to

track performance and forecast trends.

- **Finance Industry:** Banks use Data Warehouses to analyze **customer transactions, credit histories, and financial risk assessments**.

- **Advantages:**
  - High **query performance and data integrity**.
  - Ideal for **business intelligence (BI) tools** like Tableau and Power BI.

- **Limitations:**
  - **Limited scalability** due to structured storage constraints.
  - Not suitable for handling **real-time or unstructured data**.

b. Data Lakes: Flexible Storage for Raw and Unstructured Data

A **Data Lake** is a **scalable storage system** that holds **raw, unstructured, and semi-structured data** in its native format (Davenport & Dyché, 2017).

- **Key Characteristics:**
  - Stores **structured, semi-structured, and unstructured data**.
  - Uses **schema-on-read**, meaning data is stored first and processed when needed.
  - Supports **advanced analytics, machine learning, and AI** applications.

- **Use Case Example:**
  - **Healthcare Industry:** Hospitals use Data Lakes to store **electronic health records (EHRs), medical imaging, and real-time patient monitoring data**.
  - **Social Media Platforms:** Companies like **Facebook and Twitter store massive amounts of user-generated data in Data Lakes for behavioral analysis and ad targeting**.
- **Advantages:**
  - Highly **scalable and cost-effective** for large datasets.
  - Ideal for **real-time analytics and machine learning applications**.
- **Limitations:**
  - Can become a **"Data Swamp"** if not managed properly, leading to **data inconsistency and redundancy**.
  - Requires **data governance policies** to ensure data usability.

Big Data continues to reshape industries, drive innovation, and enhance operational efficiency. Organizations that successfully manage and analyze Big Data gain a competitive edge by making data-driven decisions, optimizing processes, and delivering personalized experiences. Looking ahead, emerging technologies such as Edge Computing, AI-driven Data Lakes, and Blockchain for data security will further enhance Big Data capabilities. Businesses must adopt robust data governance frameworks and invest in scalable analytics platforms to harness the full potential of Big Data.

AI and Big Data Integration in Business Intelligence

The integration of **Artificial Intelligence (AI) and Big Data** in **Business Intelligence (BI)** has revolutionized how organizations process information, gain insights, and make strategic decisions. By leveraging **machine learning algorithms, real-time analytics, and predictive modeling**, companies can optimize performance, enhance efficiency, and drive business growth.

1. The Role of Business Intelligence in Companies

Business Intelligence (BI) refers to the **processes, technologies, and tools** that transform raw data into meaningful insights for **strategic decision-making** (Chen, Chiang, & Storey, 2012). BI systems **collect, analyze, and visualize** data from multiple sources, enabling companies to improve operational efficiency and competitiveness.

Key Functions of Business Intelligence in Organizations

1. **Data Aggregation & Integration**
    - BI platforms consolidate data from multiple sources such as **ERP, CRM, marketing, and financial systems**.
    - Example: **SAP BusinessObjects integrates sales,**

customer interactions, and supply chain data for a unified dashboard.

2. **Data Analysis & Reporting**
    - BI tools **generate reports, dashboards, and key performance indicators (KPIs)** to track business performance.
    - Example: **Power BI helps executives monitor revenue trends, customer churn, and market opportunities in real time.**

3. **Predictive & Prescriptive Analytics**
    - BI systems use AI-powered analytics to **forecast trends and recommend business strategies**.
    - Example: **Retail companies predict customer demand and optimize inventory management based on historical sales data.**

4. **Customer Behavior Insights**
    - AI-driven BI systems analyze consumer preferences, social media trends, and buying patterns for targeted marketing campaigns.
    - Example: **Amazon uses AI-based BI to personalize product recommendations, leading to increased sales conversion rates.**

5. **Operational Efficiency & Cost Reduction**
    - BI tools **identify inefficiencies, optimize supply chains, and reduce operational costs**.
    - Example: **Manufacturing firms use BI to detect**

bottlenecks and optimize production schedules.

By integrating AI and Big Data into BI, companies **automate decision-making, improve business agility, and drive profitability**.

---

2. AI Utilization in Data Analytics for Decision Support

AI-powered data analytics enhances BI capabilities by automating data processing, detecting patterns, and generating insights (Davenport & Harris, 2017). The combination of AI and Big Data enables businesses to move beyond descriptive analytics to predictive and prescriptive analytics.

a. AI-Powered Predictive Analytics

- **Definition:** Uses **historical data and machine learning models** to forecast future outcomes.
- **Application:**
  - **Retail:** Predicting **customer demand** to optimize inventory.
  - **Finance:** Detecting **market trends** for better investment decisions.
  - **Healthcare:** Predicting **disease outbreaks** and patient readmission risks.
- **Example: Walmart's AI-powered demand forecasting**

system predicts seasonal sales fluctuations using Big Data analytics.

b. AI-Driven Prescriptive Analytics

- **Definition:** Provides **actionable recommendations** by analyzing multiple data points.
- **Application:**
  - **Marketing:** Suggesting personalized promotions based on customer segmentation.
  - **Supply Chain:** Optimizing logistics routes using real-time traffic data.
- **Example: UPS's ORION AI system** dynamically adjusts delivery routes, reducing fuel costs by $50 million annually.

c. Real-Time Decision-Making with AI

- **Definition:** Uses **AI models and Big Data streaming** to make instant business decisions.
- **Application:**
  - **Stock Trading:** AI algorithms **execute high-frequency trades** based on market fluctuations.
  - **Cybersecurity:** AI-powered **threat detection systems** analyze real-time data to prevent cyberattacks.
- **Example: JP Morgan Chase's AI fraud detection system** flags suspicious transactions within seconds.

d. AI-Based Natural Language Processing (NLP) in BI

- **Definition:** NLP enables BI tools to **understand, interpret, and generate human language** for business insights.
- **Application:**
  - **Sentiment Analysis:** AI analyzes **customer reviews and social media posts** to understand public perception.
  - **Automated Reporting:** AI-powered BI tools generate **business reports in natural language** for non-technical users.
- **Example: Google Cloud's AutoML NLP** extracts valuable insights from unstructured business data.

AI-driven analytics enables organizations to automate data interpretation, improve accuracy, and enhance real-time decision-making.

3. Case Studies: AI and Big Data Implementation in Leading Companies

Case Study 1: AI and Big Data in Retail – Amazon

Challenge:

Amazon needed to **optimize inventory management and improve personalized recommendations** for customers.

Solution:

Amazon integrated **AI-driven Business Intelligence** powered by **Big Data analytics, machine learning, and predictive modeling**:

- **AI-powered recommendation engine** analyzes customer **browsing history, past purchases, and reviews** to suggest products.
- **Big Data supply chain analytics** predicts demand and automates inventory restocking.
- **AI-based chatbot (Alexa)** provides customer support and voice-based shopping.

Impact:

■ **35% of Amazon's revenue** comes from AI-powered recommendations.

■ Optimized **logistics and delivery systems** reduce inventory waste.

■ Enhanced **customer experience and engagement** through AI-driven personalization.

Case Study 2: AI in Financial Services – JPMorgan Chase

Challenge:

JPMorgan Chase faced **growing threats of fraud and financial risks**, requiring **real-time fraud detection**.

Solution:

JPMorgan implemented AI-powered **Business Intelligence for fraud detection and risk assessment**:

- **AI anomaly detection algorithms** flag suspicious transactions in real time.
- **Natural Language Processing (NLP) AI** automates contract analysis, reducing manual workload.
- **Predictive analytics models** assess **credit risk and loan approvals** based on customer data.

Impact:

■ AI fraud detection reduced financial losses by **$1 billion annually**.

■ NLP-powered contract analysis cut down **manual review time from 360,000 hours to seconds**.

■ Improved **accuracy and efficiency** in financial risk management.

Case Study 3: AI in Healthcare – IBM Watson Health

Challenge:

Doctors needed **AI-powered insights** to diagnose diseases accurately and recommend treatments.

Solution:

IBM Watson Health implemented AI-driven **Big Data analytics**:

- **Machine Learning models** analyze vast amounts of **medical research papers and patient records**.
- **AI-powered diagnostics** assist doctors in predicting diseases like cancer.

- **Personalized treatment recommendations** based on patient history.

Impact:

■ **30% improvement in diagnostic accuracy** for certain diseases.

■ Faster **data analysis of 20+ million oncology studies** in minutes.

■ Enhanced **patient outcomes with AI-driven decision support**.

Key Takeaways:

✔ AI-powered BI automates data analysis, enabling faster and smarter decision-making.

✔ Big Data analytics optimizes business operations, reducing costs and increasing profitability.

✔ AI-driven BI applications will continue evolving with advancements in deep learning, NLP, and cloud computing.

As AI and Big Data technologies continue to evolve, organizations must invest in scalable AI-driven BI solutions to stay competitive in the digital economy.

Challenges and Ethical Considerations in AI and Big Data

The rapid adoption of AI and Big Data in business brings significant benefits but also introduces critical challenges and ethical concerns. Organizations must address data security, privacy issues, bias in AI algorithms, and regulatory compliance to ensure responsible and fair implementation.

---

1. Data Security and User Privacy in AI and Big Data

a. The Importance of Data Security in AI and Big Data

- **AI and Big Data systems process vast amounts of sensitive information**, including financial transactions, healthcare records, and personal user data.
- **Cybersecurity threats** such as **hacking, data breaches, and ransomware attacks** put organizations at risk of financial loss and reputational damage.
- Example: In **2017, the Equifax data breach exposed 147 million users' sensitive information**, leading to severe financial penalties.

b. Privacy Risks and Unauthorized Data Collection

- AI-powered **data analytics and tracking tools** collect personal information, often without explicit user consent.
- Example: **Facebook-Cambridge Analytica scandal (2018)** revealed how user data was exploited for political advertising, raising concerns about data privacy and ethical use.
- **AI-driven facial recognition** in public spaces raises concerns about **mass surveillance and human rights**

violations.

c. Strategies for Strengthening Data Security and Privacy

■ Data Encryption & Anonymization – Encrypting personal data ensures secure transmission and storage.

■ Multi-Factor Authentication (MFA) – Strengthens access control to prevent unauthorized access.

■ Privacy by Design – Embedding privacy controls into AI and data processing systems.

■ User Transparency & Consent Mechanisms – Organizations must clearly disclose data collection practices and allow users to control their data.

---

2. Bias in AI and Ethical Use of Big Data

a. How Bias Affects AI Decision-Making

AI systems are trained on **historical data**, which can **inadvertently reinforce discrimination and bias**. Bias in AI can result from:

1. **Data Bias** – AI models trained on biased datasets produce **unfair and inaccurate predictions**.
   - Example: **Amazon's AI hiring tool (2018) showed gender bias,** favoring male candidates due to biased historical hiring data.
2. **Algorithmic Bias** – AI decision-making models prioritize **certain groups unfairly**, leading to **discriminatory**

outcomes.

- ○ Example: **AI-powered facial recognition technology has higher error rates for people of color**, causing concerns about **racial profiling**.

3. **Human Bias in AI Development** – Developers' unconscious biases influence **how AI models are designed and trained**.

b. Ethical Concerns in Big Data Usage

Organizations leveraging Big Data must **ensure ethical use** in:

■ **Marketing & Consumer Profiling** – AI-driven **targeted ads must respect consumer rights and avoid manipulation**.

■ **Employee Monitoring** – AI in **workplace surveillance** raises privacy concerns about **tracking employee productivity**.

■ **Predictive Policing & Criminal Justice** – AI-driven predictive policing tools have been **criticized for racial bias and unfair targeting**.

c. Strategies for Reducing Bias in AI & Ensuring Ethical AI

■ **Bias Audits & Fairness Testing** – AI models should be **tested for bias** before deployment.

■ **Diverse & Inclusive Training Data** – Ensuring AI models **represent all demographics fairly**.

■ **Explainable AI (XAI)** – Making AI decision-making **transparent and interpretable**.

■ **Ethical AI Governance Frameworks** – Establishing guidelines to **hold organizations accountable** for AI bias.

Future Trends in AI and Big Data for Management Information Systems

The future of Management Information Systems (MIS) will be driven by rapid advancements in Artificial Intelligence (AI) and Big Data. As businesses continue to embrace digital transformation, AI-driven automation, real-time data analytics, and intelligent decision-making will shape how organizations operate, innovate, and remain competitive.

This section explores the latest AI technological advancements, future trends in data management and analytics, and the role of AI and Big Data in the evolution of MIS.

---

1. Latest Advancements in AI Technology

a. Explainable AI (XAI) for Transparency and Trust

- AI models, particularly **deep learning**, function as **black boxes**, making decision-making processes difficult to interpret.
- **Explainable AI (XAI)** provides **transparent insights** into how AI models reach conclusions, increasing **trust and compliance** in industries like healthcare, finance, and law.
- **Example:** IBM's AI OpenScale enables organizations to

monitor and explain AI-driven decisions to avoid biased or unethical outcomes.

b. Generative AI & Large Language Models (LLMs)

- The rise of **Generative AI** (e.g., ChatGPT, Google Bard) enables businesses to **automate content creation, customer interactions, and problem-solving**.
- **AI-powered virtual assistants** are revolutionizing **customer support, document generation, and personalized recommendations**.
- **Example:** Chatbots using **GPT-4** handle **complex business queries, automate reports, and provide real-time insights**.

c. AI-Powered Automation and Hyperautomation

- **Hyper Automation** combines AI, **Robotic Process Automation (RPA)**, and machine learning to **automate end-to-end business processes**.
- Businesses use **AI-driven automation** to enhance **workforce productivity and reduce operational costs**.
- **Example:** UiPath's AI-powered **RPA bots** automate **invoice processing, HR recruitment, and customer service interactions**.

d. AI in Edge Computing for Real-Time Processing

- **Edge AI** enables **real-time AI processing on local devices** instead of relying on cloud-based AI models.

- This reduces **latency, enhances security, and improves speed**, particularly in **IoT, smart cities, and autonomous vehicles**.

- **Example:** Tesla's self-driving AI processes **real-time traffic data on the vehicle** instead of sending it to the cloud.

e. AI-Powered Cybersecurity for Threat Detection

- AI-driven cybersecurity solutions **detect and prevent cyber threats in real time**.

- AI-based **anomaly detection** monitors network traffic for **suspicious behavior and fraud detection**.

- **Example:** Darktrace's AI-powered security platform autonomously detects and mitigates **cyber threats in enterprises**.

---

2. Future Trends in Data Management and Analytics

a. Real-Time and Streaming Data Analytics

- Traditional batch processing is being replaced by **real-time data processing**, allowing businesses to make **instant data-driven decisions**.

- AI-powered streaming analytics is used in **finance, healthcare, e-commerce, and logistics**.

- **Example:** Nasdaq's AI-driven stock trading platform analyzes **millions of transactions per second** for fraud detection and automated trading.

b. AI-Driven Data Lakes and Warehouses

- **Data Lakes** and **Data Warehouses** are evolving into **AI-powered Data Management Systems**, enabling **automated data classification, cleansing, and governance**.
- AI ensures **better data quality, compliance, and security**.
- **Example:** Snowflake's AI-enhanced cloud **Data Warehouse** optimizes **data storage, retrieval, and analytics**.

c. Federated Learning for Privacy-Preserving AI

- **Federated learning** enables AI models to **train on decentralized data sources** without sharing sensitive information.
- This method enhances **privacy in healthcare, finance, and autonomous systems**.
- **Example:** Google's **AI-powered mobile keyboard (Gboard)** uses **federated learning** to improve typing predictions without storing user data in the cloud.

d. AI-Driven Data Governance and Compliance

- With stricter regulations (e.g., GDPR, CCPA), businesses use AI for **automated data compliance, monitoring, and**

auditing.

- AI ensures **data security, prevents unauthorized access, and automates compliance reporting**.
- **Example:** IBM Cloud Pak for Data helps enterprises comply with **privacy laws by classifying and securing sensitive information**.

---

3. The Future of Management Information Systems with AI and Big Data

The integration of **AI and Big Data** will redefine **Management Information Systems (MIS)** by making them **more intelligent, automated, and real-time**.

a. Autonomous MIS for AI-Driven Decision Making

- **AI-powered MIS** will evolve into **self-learning, autonomous decision-making systems**.
- **MIS will analyze vast datasets, identify patterns, and recommend business strategies with minimal human intervention**.
- **Example:** AI-powered **ERP systems** will dynamically **adjust business operations based on real-time market trends**.

b. AI-Powered Business Intelligence for Competitive Advantage

- AI-driven **BI platforms** will provide real-time dashboards with **predictive and prescriptive insights**.
- Businesses will move beyond descriptive analytics to **automated, AI-driven strategic planning**.
- **Example:** AI-powered **Google Looker and Microsoft Power BI** will enable enterprises to **automatically detect risks, trends, and business opportunities**.

c. Human-AI Collaboration in Decision Support Systems

- AI **augments human intelligence** by providing **data-driven recommendations**, but humans will still **make final strategic decisions**.
- **Example:** AI-driven **HR systems** will suggest **employee training programs**, but HR leaders will make final **promotion and hiring decisions**.

d. AI in Sustainable and Green Computing for MIS

- AI and Big Data will be used for **optimizing energy consumption, reducing carbon footprints, and promoting sustainability in IT infrastructure**.
- AI-driven **cloud computing solutions** will dynamically allocate computing resources **to minimize power usage**.
- **Example:** Google's **AI-driven data centers** reduced **energy consumption by 40%**, improving environmental sustainability.

e. AI and Quantum Computing for Next-Gen MIS

- **Quantum AI** will revolutionize data processing by solving complex business problems **exponentially faster than classical computing.**
- Industries such as **finance, pharmaceuticals, and supply chain logistics** will leverage **quantum-enhanced AI models.**
- **Example:** IBM's **Quantum AI research** explores real-world applications for **financial modeling and cryptography.**

The future of Management Information Systems is AI-powered, data-driven, and highly automated. AI and Big Data will transform how organizations collect, analyze, and utilize information for competitive advantage.

Key Takeaways:

✔ **AI and Big Data will enable real-time, autonomous decision-making in business operations.**
✔ **AI-driven analytics will enhance predictive modeling, fraud detection, and strategic planning.**
✔ **AI-powered cloud computing and edge AI will revolutionize enterprise data processing.**
✔ **The evolution of MIS will integrate human-AI collaboration, ensuring ethical and fair AI implementation.**

As AI and Big Data continue to shape the future, organizations that adopt these technologies strategically will thrive in the next era of intelligent digital transformation.

ABOUT AUTHORS

 Rike Setiawati, born in Jambi on April 3, 1962, is a figure who not only develops through time, but also through knowledge and dedication. With a Bachelor of Economics degree from the Faculty of Economics, Jambi University in 1988, Rike has started her long journey in the academic world.

As the seventh child of Mrs. Sutiem and Mr. William Siem Lamsang, Rike continued to pursue her dreams. Not just stopping at the undergraduate level, she continued her Master's studies at the Master of Management Faculty of Economics, Jambi University, completing it brilliantly in 2003. Her extraordinary dedication was also seen when she earned her Doctorate degree from the Doctor of Management Science study program at Padjadjaran University Bandung in 2018.

Her academic journey is not only reflected in the degrees she holds, but also in her leadership experience. Rike was once the head of the Management department of the Jambi University FEB Extension program, and now carries the responsibility as the head of the Entrepreneurship study program at Jambi University FEB. In 2012, she was also a member of the senate of Jambi University, contributing significantly to academic development.

However, Rike's achievements are not limited to formal academia. A number of researches in the field of financial management and entrepreneurship have been successfully completed by her. Her brilliant articles have been published in various National and International journals, reflecting her contribution to the development of science.

In addition, Rike Setiawati is an active figure in community service activities. As an instructor and resource person, she has shared her knowledge and experience in various training activities, both at the government, private, and university levels. Her experience as a teacher is not only limited to the scope of higher education, but also includes teaching at Purnama Jambi High School and SMEA, Jambi Batanghari University, and Jambi Muhammadiyah University.

Since February 1989 until now, Rike Setiawati has remained loyal as an active lecturer at the Faculty of Economics and Business, Jambi University. Her tireless dedication, in-depth knowledge, and burning passion make Rike Setiawati an inspiring figure in the academic world.

If you would like to contact Rike Setiawati for more information or collaboration, here are the contacts:

Email   rike_setiawati@unja.ac.id

 Andy Ismail is an inspiring figure, with a rich background in business and literature. As CEO of PT Asadel Liamsindo Teknologi, he has made his mark in the software as a service (SaaS) industry and Artificial Intelligence (AI) development. His partnerships with renowned global and local technology companies mark his strong commitment to collaboration and innovation.

However, his achievements are not just limited to the business world. Andy Ismail is also known as a talented writer, with his books providing insights into digital transformation and preparing to be a startup founder. The book "Leading the Digital Transformation: Evidence from Indonesia" provides valuable insights into the importance of digital leadership in this era of transformation.

His expertise in computer science, especially in various programming languages and web technologies, adds weight to his profile as a competent technology leader and practitioner. His long experience in business also reflects his success in networking and gaining deserved recognition.

Not only that, Andy Ismail is also a lecturer at Darwan Ali University. On top of that, he is also a practicing lecturer at Jambi University, sharing his first-hand experience to the eager young generation. His LinkedIn profile will give you a more complete picture of his outstanding achievements and contributions.

Here are the contacts that can be reached:

Email   andy@unda.ac.id, ceo@asadel.co.id

 Herzalina Herbenita is a distinguished scholar in the field of financial management, currently serving at Universitas Darwan Ali. With an impressive academic background and a commitment to excellence, Herzalina has made significant contributions to understanding financial fraud and corporate financial health.

Her academic journey is highlighted by her research on fraud detection using the Fraud Triangle and Beneish Model, which has been recognized and published in various reputable journals. Notable among her publications is the article titled "Potential of Fraud Financial Statements: The Fraud Triangle," published in the Central Asian Journal of Innovations on Tourism Management and Finance in 2022. Her other significant work includes "ANALISIS FRAUD TRIANGLE DALAM MENDETEKSI POTENSI KECURANGAN LAPORAN KEUANGAN MENGGUNAKAN BENEISH MODEL," showcasing her expertise in leveraging advanced models for fraud detection.

In addition to her focus on fraud detection, Herzalina has explored the impact of financial ratios and company size on financial distress conditions. Her collaborative work, "Analisis Pengaruh Rasio Keuangan dan Ukuran Perusahaan Terhadap Kondisi Financial Distress (Studi Pada Perusahaan Industri Dasar dan Kimia di Bursa Efek Indonesia Tahun 2014-2017)," co-authored with R. Kusumawati, offers valuable insights into the financial health of industrial companies in Indonesia.

Herzalina's contributions to the field are marked by her rigorous research methodologies and her ability to translate complex financial concepts into practical applications. Her work not only advances academic knowledge but also provides actionable insights for practitioners in the field of financial management.

Herzalina Herbenita's dedication to research and her impactful publications make her a respected authority in financial management, and her work continues to inspire and inform professionals and academics alike.

Here are the contacts that can be reached:

Email   herbenita@unda.ac.id

 **Bambang Sutejo** is an academic and researcher with a strong background in business and economic studies. He holds a Master's degree in Management from Krisnadwipayana University and a Bachelor's degree in Economics, majoring in Management, from Jenderal Soedirman University. Currently, he serves as a lecturer at the Faculty of Business, Darwan Ali University, where he shares his expertise in management and economic principles. Additionally, he is actively engaged in research at the Center for Socio-Economic Studies in Jember, focusing on economic and social policy analysis. His academic and professional pursuits reflect a deep commitment to advancing knowledge in business and economics.

For inquiries, he can be reached at **tejosampit@gmail.com** or **bambang.sutejo@ms.unda.ac.id**.

 **Sigit Mulyanto** is an academic and accounting expert with extensive experience in education and taxation. He holds a Master's degree in Accounting from Budi Luhur University and a Bachelor's degree in Economic Education with a specialization in Accounting Education from Sebelas Maret University. Currently, he is a lecturer at the Faculty of Business, Darwan Ali University, where he imparts his knowledge in accounting and finance. In addition to his role as an educator, he serves as the Head of the Tax Center at Darwan Ali University, actively contributing to tax education and research. His dedication to accounting and taxation reflects his commitment to developing financial literacy and academic excellence.

For inquiries, he can be reached at **sigitmul@gmail.com** or **smulyanto@unda.ac.id**.

ADDITIONAL AUTHORS

Muhammad Aqshal Zorif

Muhammad Aqshal Zorif is a dedicated student currently pursuing a Bachelor's degree in Entrepreneurship at Universitas Jambi, Indonesia. Aqshal is passionate about the principles of entrepreneurship and is eager to apply his academic knowledge to real-world business challenges. His studies focus on understanding the fundamentals of business development, innovation, and sustainable practices, preparing him for a future in the entrepreneurial world.

Mustika Sari

Mustika Sari is an enthusiastic student of Entrepreneurship at Universitas Jambi, Indonesia. With a keen interest in social entrepreneurship and community development, Mustika is committed to learning how to leverage business skills to address social issues. Her academic journey is enriched by her involvement in projects that aim to empower local communities and promote sustainable development through entrepreneurial initiatives.

Uswatun Hasanah

Uswatun Hasanah is a proactive student of Entrepreneurship at Universitas Jambi, Indonesia. Her academic interests include digital entrepreneurship and e-commerce, areas she believes hold significant potential for future business opportunities. Uswatun is dedicated to acquiring the skills and knowledge necessary to navigate the rapidly evolving digital marketplace, with the aim of contributing to innovative business solutions in the future.

Della Adelia

Della Adelia is a committed student of Entrepreneurship at Universitas Jambi, Indonesia. Her focus is on the creative industries, where she explores how entrepreneurship can foster the growth of art, culture, and local crafts. Through her studies, Della aims to develop strategies that support the sustainability and economic viability of creative enterprises, blending her passion for the arts with sound business practices.

Ghani Akbar

Ghani Akbar is a dedicated student currently studying Entrepreneurship at Universitas Jambi, Indonesia. He is particularly interested in startup development and venture capital. Ghani is focused on understanding the intricacies of launching and growing new ventures, and his academic work is geared towards gaining insights into effective startup management and funding strategies.

These additional authors, all students from the Entrepreneurship program at Universitas Jambi, Indonesia, bring a fresh and diverse perspective to the field of entrepreneurship. Their academic endeavors and collaborative spirit reflect their commitment to learning and their potential to become future leaders in the business world.

REFERENCES

Books and Journal Articles:

Anderson, R., & Moore, T. (2006). The economics of information security. *Science, 314*(5799), 610-613.

Arbie, E. (2015). *Pengantar sistem informasi.* Gramedia.

Bishop, M. (2018). *Computer security: Art and science* (2nd ed.). Addison-Wesley.

Debbyanti, F. (2013). *Sistem informasi pembelian, penjualan, dan pendistribusian keramik accura berbasis website pada PT SAMAJAYASUKSESABADI.*

Fruhlinger, J. (2020). Equifax data breach FAQ: What happened, who was affected, what was the impact? *CSO Online.*

Hall, J. A. (2016). *Accounting information systems* (9th ed.). Cengage Learning.

Hidayatun, N., Marlina, S., & Adinata, E. (2020). Perancangan sistem inventory untuk pengelolaan data persediaan bahan baku.

Hinson, G. (2018). *Security risk assessment: Managing and conducting.* CRC Press.

Jacobs, F. R., & Chase, R. B. (2017). *Manufacturing planning and control for supply chain management.* McGraw-Hill.

Kertahadi, K. (2010). *Sistem informasi dalam manajemen.* Mitra Wacana Media.

Khristianto, W., Supriyanto, T., & Wahyuni, S. (2015). *Sistem informasi manajemen (Pendekatan sosioteknik).*

Kotler, P., & Keller, K. L. (2016). *Marketing management.* Pearson.

Laudon, K. C., & Laudon, J. P. (2018). *Management information systems: Managing the digital firm* (15th ed.). Pearson.

McLeod, R., & Schell, G. (2007). *Sistem informasi manajemen.* Salemba Empat.

Muhairia, A., & Novitarina, D. A. (2010). Sistem informasi manajemen penjualan, pembelian dan persediaan pada PT. Romindo Palembang.

Muhyuzir, T. D. (2014). *Manajemen sistem informasi.* Elex Media Komputindo.

Mufidah, Z. (2017). Penerapan matriks strategis sistem informasi: Studi kasus di Dinas Perpustakaan Umum dan Arsip Daerah (DPAD) Kota Malang. *BIBLIOTIKA: Jurnal Kajian Perpustakaan dan Informasi, 1*, 10.17977/um008v1i12017p058.

Nadia Kurniati, A., & Devitra, J. (2022). Sistem informasi administrasi keuangan siswa berbasis web pada SMA Yadika Kota Jambi. *Jurnal Manajemen Sistem Informasi*.

Perlroth, IN. (2021). *This is how they tell me the world ends: The cyber-weapons arms race*. Bloomsbury Publishing.

Pfleeger, C. P., Pfleeger, S. L., & Margulies, J. (2015). *Security in computing* (5th ed.). Prentice Hall.

Pressman, R. S. (2014). *Software engineering: A practitioner's approach* (8th ed.). McGraw-Hill.

Rifai, M., & Sarono, J. (2014). Sistem informasi medical check up CTKI Klinik Mitra Mutiara. *Jurnal CoSciTech (Computer Science and Information Technology)*.

Romney, M. B., & Steinbart, P. J. (2015). *Accounting information systems* (13th ed.). Pearson Education.

Sani, A., & Ratih, R. (2010). Sistem informasi manajemen penjualan, persediaan dan pembelian pada PT. Karya

Suka Abadi Palembang.

Scarfone, K., & Mell, P. (2007). Guide to intrusion detection and prevention systems (IDPS). *NIST Special Publication 800-94.*

Solove, D. J., & Schwartz, P. M. (2020). *Information privacy law.* Aspen Publishers.

Stallings, W., & Brown, L. (2018). *Computer security: Principles and practice.* Pearson Education.

Sutabri, T. (2012). *Sistem informasi manajemen.* Andi Offset.

Turban, E., Outland, J., King, D., Lee, J., & Liang, T. (2005). *Electronic commerce 2006: A managerial perspective.* Prentice Hall.

Wahyudin, I., Natsir, F., & Vandini, I. (2022). Perancangan aplikasi sistem informasi penjualan tahu pada Pabrik Tahu UG Pariangan berbasis Java. *Jurnal Aplikasi Teknologi Informasi dan Manajemen (JATIM).*

Whitman, M. E., & Mattord, H. J. (2022). *Principles of information security.* Cengage Learning.

Chapter 10:

Brynjolfsson, E., & McAfee, A. (2017). *Machine, Platform, Crowd: Harnessing Our Digital Future*. W. W. Norton & Company.

Davenport, T. H., & Ronanki, R. (2018). Artificial Intelligence for the Real World. *Harvard Business Review*, 96(1), 108-116.

Marr, B. (2018). *Big Data in Practice: How 45 Successful Companies Used Big Data Analytics to Deliver Extraordinary Results*. Wiley.

Russell, S. J., & Norvig, P. (2021). *Artificial Intelligence: A Modern Approach* (4th ed.). Pearson.

Witten, I. H., Frank, E., Hall, M. A., & Pal, C. J. (2016). *Data Mining: Practical Machine Learning Tools and Techniques* (4th ed.). Morgan Kaufmann.

Websites:

https://accurate.id/marketing-manajemen/sistem-informasi-sdm/

https://askerisoft.com/aplikasi-departement-sdm/

https://blog.gamatechno.com/7-software-hr-terbaik-untuk-sistem-informasi-kepegawaian/?amp=1

https://dokodemo-kerja.com/blog/ind/info-hrd/sistem-informasi-sumber-daya-manusia/

https://dokodemo-kerja.com/blog/ind/info-hris/software-hr/

https://www.academia.edu/40111374/Buku_Ajar_SISTEM_INFORMASI_MANAJEMEN

https://www.studocu.com/id/document/universitas-mulawarman/komputer

www.ingramcontent.com/pod-product-compliance
Lightning Source LLC
LaVergne TN
LVHW051344050326
832903LV00031B/3724